Object Lessons
That Teach Bible Verses

Object Lessons Series

Bess, C. W., *Children's Object Sermons for the Seasons,* 1026-8

Bess, C. W., *Object-Centered Children's Sermons,* 0734-8

Bess, C. W., *Sparkling Object Sermons for Children,* 0824-7

Bess, C. W., & Roy DeBrand, *Bible-Centered Object Sermons for Children,* 0886-7

Biller, Tom & Martie, *Simple Object Lessons for Children,* 0793-3

Bruinsma, Sheryl, *Easy-to-Use Object Lessons,* 0832-8

Bruinsma, Sheryl, *More Object Lessons for Very Young Children,* 1075-6

Bruinsma, Sheryl, *New Object Lessons,* 0775-5

Bruinsma, Sheryl, *Object Lessons for Every Occasion,* 0994-4

Bruinsma, Sheryl, *Object Lessons for Special Days,* 0920-0

Bruinsma, Sheryl, *Object Lessons for Very Young Children,* 0956-1

Bruinsma, Sheryl, *Object Lessons Using Children's Toys,* 5695-0

Claassen, David, *Object Lessons for a Year,* 2514-1

Connelly, H. W., *47 Object Lessons for Youth Programs,* 2314-9

Coombs, Robert, *Concise Object Sermons for Children,* 2541-9

Coombs, Robert, *Enlightening Object Lessons for Children,* 2567-2

Cooper, Charlotte, *50 Object Stories for Children,* 2523-0

Cross, Luther, *Easy Object Stories,* 2502-8

Cross, Luther, *Object Lessons for Children,* 2315-7

Cross, Luther, *Story Sermons for Children,* 2328-9

De Jonge, Joanne, *More Object Lessons from Nature,* 3004-8

De Jonge, Joanne, *Object Lessons from Nature,* 2989-9

De Jonge, Joanne, *Object Lessons from Pebbles and Paper Clips,* 5041-3

De Jonge, Joanne, *Object Lessons from Your Home and Yard,* 3026-9

Edstrom, Lois, *Contemporary Object Lessons for Children's Church,* 3432-9

Gebhardt, Richard & Mark Armstrong, *Object Lessons from Science Experiments,* 3811-1

Godsey, Kyle, *Object Lessons About God,* 3841-3

Hendricks, William, *Object Lessons Based on Bible Characters,* 4373-5

Hendricks, William, & Merle Den Bleyker, *Object Lessons from Sports and Games,* 4134-1

Hendricks, William, & Merle Den Bleyker, *Object Lessons That Teach Bible Truths,* 4172-4

Loeks, Mary, *Object Lesson for Children's Worship,* 5584-9

McDonald, Roderick, *Successful Object Sermons,* 6270-5

Runk, Wesley, *Object Lessons from the Bible,* 7698-6

Squyres, Greg, *Simple Object Lessons for Young Children,* 8330-3

Sullivan, Jessie, *Object Lessons and Stories for Children's Church,* 8037-1

Sullivan, Jessie, *Object Lessons with Easy-to-Find Objects,* 8190-4

Trull, Joe, *40 Object Sermons for Children,* 8831-3

Object Lessons
That Teach Bible Verses

William Hendricks

Baker Books

A Division of Baker Book House Co
Grand Rapids, Michigan 49516

Published by Baker Books
a division of Baker Book House Company
P.O. Box 6287, Grand Rapids, MI 49516-6287

Printed in the United States of America

ISBN 0-8010-4278-X

For current information about all releases from Baker Book House,
visit our web site:

http://www.bakerbooks.com

Contents

Part One
Learning about God

1

Hiding God's Word in Your Heart

Concept: Learning Bible verses helps us to keep away from sin.

Objects: Cherries with pits

Memory Verse: Psalm 119:11—I have hidden your word in my heart that I might not sin against you.

Do you know what these are? *(Show the cherries. Allow responses.)* Right; they're nice, ripe cherries. How many of you like to eat cherries? *(Allow responses.)* When you eat cherries you have to be careful because something is inside of them. Do you know what's inside? *(Allow responses.)* Right! Every cherry has a pit inside. A cherry pit isn't good to eat, but it is very important. A cherry pit is really the seed of a cherry tree. If you want a new cherry tree to grow, you have to plant a cherry pit. Even though you can't see the pit from the outside, God made it to be a very important part of the cherry.

We have important parts inside of us too. We have hearts and minds to help us learn and remember things.

We can learn important verses from the Bible. We can store them inside of us, in our hearts, so that we can use them to help us live for Jesus. Knowing what the Bible tells us to do keeps us from doing what God doesn't want us to do. Knowing God's Word helps us to keep from sinning against God.

Today I have a verse for you to learn that reminds us of cherry pits. It tells us that what is inside of us is really important.

The verse we want to learn together today is Psalm 119:11. It says, "I have hidden your word in my heart that I might not sin against you."

I'll say the first part, and you say it after me. Then I'll say the rest, and you say that back to me just like an echo. After that we'll ask our moms and dads and everyone else to say it all together with us. Ready? "I have hidden your word in my heart" *(encourage children to echo phrase)* "that I might not sin against you." *(Children echo.)* Psalm 119, verse 11. *(Children echo.)* Now everyone. *(Lead all in saying verse and location.)*

Whenever you look at a cherry *(hold up cherry)*, think about the pit that's inside. Remember how important it is to have God's Word hidden in your heart so that you do not sin against God.

2

Being Shaped
to Be More like Jesus

Concept: Learning God's way can shape us to become more like Jesus.

Objects: Muffin tin, some batter, and a muffin

Memory Verse: Psalm 86:11—Teach me your way, O LORD, and I will walk in your truth.

One of the things I really like to eat is a hot muffin. To make muffins, you need a pan like this. *(Hold up the one you have.)* This muffin pan has hollow spots in it like a row of little cups. Can anyone tell me what all these hollow spots are for? *(Allow responses.)* I suppose that your mother or father fries eggs in a pan with a flat bottom. Why can't you use a pan with a flat bottom to make muffins? *(Allow responses.)* Right! If I take this muffin batter *(stir and show it to the children)* and bake it in a flat pan, it wouldn't be shaped like this *(hold up a baked muffin)* at all. A muffin gets its shape from the pan it was baked in. When the pan gets warm in the oven, the batter gets bigger. Then when it's all done, you can't change its shape anymore.

Something like that happens to us too. Every day we grow up just a little bit. Every day we learn and do some things that help to shape us or make us grow inside.

If the things you learn and do while you are growing up are Christian things, they help you to be a Christian all your life. That's why it's so important to learn about Jesus and try to do what he wants you to do every day.

There's a verse in the Bible that will help us remember to walk in God's way. It is Psalm 86:11. It says, "Teach me your way, O Lord, and I will walk in your truth."

I'll say the first part, and you say it after me. Then I'll say the rest, and you say that back to me just like an echo. After that we'll ask our moms and dads and everyone else to say it all together with us. Ready? "Teach me your way, O Lord" *(encourage children to echo phrase),* "and I will walk in your truth." *(Children echo.)* Psalm 86, verse 11. *(Children echo.)* Now everyone. *(Lead all in saying verse and location.)*

Whenever you see or eat a muffin, remember that the muffin got its shape from the muffin pan. *(Hold up the muffin and pan.)* As you grow up, be happy that others who love Jesus teach you and shape you to be a Christian.

3

Be Still

Concept: Quietness helps bring us close to God.

Objects: A drum and drumsticks

Memory Verse: Psalm 46:10—Be still, and know that I am God.

Listen to this. *(Beat the drum loudly.)* Do you like that kind of noise? *(Allow responses.)* Playing a drum is not only fun, but it can make a lot of noise too. What other kinds of things make a lot of noise? *(Allow responses.)* Right! There are many, many things. You could bang together pots and pans to make noise. Some places are noisy. Airports or factories with lots of machines are noisy all the time. Many of the people who work in such noisy places wear earplugs in their ears to protect their ears from the loud noise. Otherwise the noise could make them lose their ability to hear.

Have you ever gone to a really noisy ball game? *(Allow responses.)* Everyone yells to encourage the team. The cheerleaders lead the fans in cheers for their team. Maybe the band is playing too. Sometimes the noise gets so loud that you can hardly hear what the person next to you is saying.

We also can't hear what another person is saying if we ourselves are talking all the time. To hear them we have to stop talking.

The Bible doesn't tell us that we can't make any noise. It doesn't say that we mustn't talk and that we have to listen all the time.

But trying to talk to God and listen to his Word in a noisy place doesn't work very well. There are too many sounds that keep us from really praying and listening to his Word. In Psalm 46:10 the Bible tells us something very important. It says, "Be still, and know that I am God." Let's use that short verse for our memory work today.

I'll say it, and then you say it after me just like an echo. Then we'll ask our moms and dads and everyone else to say it all together with us. Ready? "Be still, and know that I am God." *(Encourage children to say verse.)* Psalm 46, verse 10. *(Children echo.)* Now everyone. *(Lead all in saying verse and location.)*

That wonderful verse tells us an important way we can get to know God better. We can just be quiet *(push away drum and drumsticks)* and listen to what he tells us in the Bible. That's why we are quiet when our parents and teachers tell us Bible stories. That's why we listen quietly when the minister reads the Bible and explains it to us. That's why we're quiet when others pray. That's why we quietly come to God in prayer ourselves. When we're quiet, when we're still, we can learn about God more quickly and praise him more easily.

God Knows the Future

Concept: We need to plan, but God's plan comes first.

Object: Plan book or planning calendar

Memory Verse: James 4:15—You ought to say, "If it is the Lord's will, we will live and do this or that."

This is my plan book/calendar, boys and girls. *(Hold up the book.)* I write lots of things in it. What kinds of things do you think I have written in it? *(Allow responses.)* Yes, I even wrote down a dentist appointment. *(Show the page.)* If I didn't write appointment dates and times in my plan book, I'd probably forget to go. Planning ahead is important, or we'd get our times mixed up. I don't have to plan for yesterday because it happened already. Why do I have to plan for tomorrow and next week? *(Allow responses.)* Right. Tomorrow is still coming. We have to do the best we can to be ready for it even though we don't know what really will happen.

Who is the only one who really knows what will happen tomorrow? *(Allow responses.)* That's right, only God knows what will really happen, not just tomorrow, but all the days after that too. Sometimes when we make our plans we think we know what is best, but God may have a better plan for us. Have you ever looked forward to going on a picnic you had planned, and then on the day of the picnic, it rained so hard you couldn't go at all? *(Allow responses.)* Or maybe your grandparents were coming to visit, and then the day they were coming one of them got sick, so the whole trip had to be canceled. *(Allow responses.)* God made the plans change.

In James 4:15 the Bible tells us something we always need to remember when we make plans. It says, "You ought to say, 'If it is the Lord's will, we will live and do this or that.'" Let's learn that special verse today.

I'll say the first part, and you say it after me. Then I'll say the rest, and you say that back to me just like an echo. After that we'll ask our moms and dads and everyone else to say it all together with us. Ready? "You ought to say, 'If it is the Lord's will' *(encourage children to echo phrase),* 'we will live and do this or that.'" *(Children echo.)* James 4, verse 15. *(Children echo.)* Now everyone. *(Lead all in saying verse and location.)*

We need to make the best plans we can, boys and girls *(hold up the book),* but we always need to remember that God is the master planner. He holds our lives and all that we do in his watchful care. In our church bulletin when we announce some big important thing we are planning to do, we often put in the letters *D.V.* That means, "If the Lord wills." Sometimes if we plan to do something and God changes our plans so that we can't do what we planned to do, we may be really disappointed. Then we have to remember that God knows the future. Don't forget that the next time this happens to you. Thank God for his perfect plans.

How Great God Is!

Concept: We see how great God is by looking at what he has made.

Objects: Handful of sand, telescope

Memory Verse: Psalm 19:1—The heavens declare the glory of God; the skies proclaim the work of his hands.

When the sky is cloudy or if there are lots of other bright lights around, it's quite hard to see the stars at night. But if it's a clear night and you go away from the city lights, you can see the stars. How many stars do you think there are? *(Allow responses.)* Yes, there are so many we can't count them all.

Now I'd like to have you look at this plastic bag of sand that I brought today. *(Hold up the sand.)* It's nice and fine. Each little grain of sand is really small. Then think of all the sand in a sandbox or on the seashore. Do you think a person could count how many grains of sand there are in the world? *(Allow responses.)* There are just too many to count.

If you looked at the night sky, even with a telescope like this *(show them yours),* you couldn't count all the stars. The telescope helps to bring them closer, but there are too many to count, even if you look with the biggest telescope in the whole world.

When you try to count the grains of sand on the seashore or the stars in the sky, then you start to understand how great God is. When you look at the night sky, you wonder how God placed all the stars up there and how he keeps them where they are supposed to be. Long ago when King David was still a shepherd boy tending his father's sheep, he looked up at those same stars and wrote a beautiful psalm about them. Psalm 19:1 says, "The heavens declare the glory of God; the skies proclaim the work of his hands." Let's learn those words of praise to God today.

I'll say the first part, and you say it after me. Then I'll say the rest, and you say that back to me just like an echo. After that we'll ask our moms and dads and everyone else to say it all together with us. Ready? "The heavens declare the glory of God" *(encourage children to echo phrase);* "the skies proclaim the work of his hands." *(Children echo.)* Psalm 19, verse 1. *(Children echo.)* Now everyone. *(Lead all in saying verse and location.)*

When we look up at the sky and see the stars we begin to feel how big God is. *(Hold up the telescope.)* When we try to count the millions and millions of tiny little grains of sand, we wonder how God could make it all. *(Hold up the sand.)* Praise our wonderful God!

Part Two
God's Love

God's Forgiveness

Concept: When God forgives our sins, they're all gone.

Objects: A small chalkboard, chalk, eraser

Memory Verse: Psalm 103:12—As far as the east is from the west, so far has he removed our transgressions from us.

Y ou all know that this is a chalkboard, don't you? *(Allow responses.)* And this is a piece of chalk. What can I do with the chalk? *(Allow responses.)* Yes, just look. *(Make lines, draw a simple picture, or print a few letters.)* Now who can erase the chalkboard for me? *(Select a volunteer.)* Now the board is clear again, isn't it?

Does someone else want to draw something on the chalkboard? *(Allow another child to make a simple picture. After praising it, allow another child to erase the board.)* Now I have a question for you. Where did the pictures and lines that were on the board go? *(Allow responses.)* Yes, they're all gone. That's just what happens to our sins when Jesus forgives us. When the Bible talks about our sins, it sometimes calls our sins "transgressions." That means that when we sin, we transgress, that is, we go beyond the limits that God sets for us in his Word.

The Bible tells us that if we pray to Jesus and ask him to forgive our sins, he takes them all away. They're all gone just like all the lines on the chalkboard were gone after we erased them.

Jesus loves us so much that he died on the cross to pay for all our sins. When you go outdoors and if you look toward the east, where the sun comes up, and then if you look as far as you can toward the west, where the sun goes down, you will know how very far Jesus takes our sins away from us.

Let's learn to say this Bible verse together today: "As far as the east is from the west, so far has he removed our transgressions from us" Psalm 103:12.

I'll say the first part, and you say it after me. Then I'll say the rest, and you say that back to me just like an echo. Then we'll ask all our moms and dads and everyone else to say it all together with us. Ready? "As far as the east is from the west" *(encourage children to echo phrase),* "so far has he removed our transgressions from us." *(Children echo.)* Psalm 103, verse 12. *(Children echo.)* Now everyone. *(Lead all in saying verse and location.)*

Each time you erase something from a chalkboard or see someone else do so *(demonstrate),* remember that God really does forgive our sins and when he does they're really all gone. They are as far away from us as the sunrise is from the sunset. That's wonderful.

7

God Knows Us All by Name

Concept: God knows each one of us.

Object: A telephone book

Memory Verse: Revelation 20:12—Another
book was opened, which is the book of life.

Do you know what this is? *(Hold up your
telephone book. Allow responses.)* Right! and if I want to
talk on the telephone to someone like (name of child
in the group)'s parents what do I have to do first?
(Allow responses.) Right again. I have to find their
telephone number in the telephone book. Let's do
that. But how are we going to find the (family
name)'s name in this big book of names? *(Allow
responses.)* Yes, and since the (family name)'s family
name starts with the letter (first letter), we'll just turn
to the (first letter)'s. *(Do so.)* Now we can find their
last name; here it is. *(Point to it.)*

Now what do we need to know? *(Allow responses.)*
Yes, we need to know the first name or initial of
(child's name)'s parents because there are quite a
few (family name)s. *(Read a number of the first names
you find listed under the family name until you get to
the right one.)* There it is. *(Read last and first name of*

child's parents as listed in the telephone book.) Their telephone number is (number). So now I can call them on the telephone. Look at all of the numbers in the telephone book. *(Hold up the book and page through it so they can see the columns.)* Every one of the numbers is different from all the others. If I make just one mistake when I call the (family name)'s number, if I dial a 4 instead of a 6, or a 7 instead of a 9, the telephone will not ring in the (family name)'s house; it will ring in somebody else's house instead. It would be the wrong number.

The Bible talks about a different kind of book. It's called the Book of Life. God keeps this book. In his book are the names of all the people who love Jesus. God doesn't get the numbers mixed up. He knows his children one by one.

There's a verse in the Bible that tells us about the Book of Life. It's Revelation 20:12. Someday that book will be opened and all the people whose names are written there will be with Jesus in heaven forever and ever.

Let's learn that verse this morning. It says, "Another book was opened, which is the book of life."

I'll say the first part, and you say it after me. Then I'll say the rest, and you say that back to me just like an echo. After that we'll ask our moms and dads and everyone else to say it all together with us. Ready? "Another book was opened" *(encourage children to echo phrase),* "which is the book of life." *(Children echo.)* Revelation 20, verse 12. *(Children echo.)* Now everyone. *(Lead all in saying verse and location.)*

Telephone books have lots of names, and every name has a different telephone number. *(Hold up the telephone book.)* We could never remember them all. But God knows all of his children. If you love Jesus, your name is written in God's Book of Life. That's something to be truly happy about today.

Taking the Wrinkles Out

Concept: God disciplines his children to help them be better Christians.

Objects: Two handkerchiefs, one wrinkled and the other ironed; an iron

Memory Verse: Hebrews 12:10—God disciplines us for our good, that we may share in his holiness.

Today I have two handkerchiefs with me. *(Hold them up.)* Can you tell me what is different about the way they look? *(Allow responses.)* Right! This one is all wrinkled and this one is nice and smooth. I put them in the washing machine together. Why do you suppose they are so different now? *(Allow responses.)* Yes. One is ironed and the other one isn't. When you iron something *(pick up your iron and show the temperature buttons),* you need to have a hot iron. You also have to press down while you're ironing. *(Illustrate.)* If you were a handkerchief would you like to get ironed? *(Allow responses.)* If I were a handkerchief I wouldn't like to get ironed either. But it's still the best way to get the wrinkles out. In some ways all of us are like this wrinkled handkerchief. *(Hold it up.)* Even though Jesus washed away our sins when he died on the cross for us, we still have lots of sins or wrinkles in our lives. Then God uses the things that happen to us from day to day to help iron out the wrinkles. *(Hold up the ironed handkerchief.)* God may send sickness. Sometimes he uses troubles and sorrow. In the Old Testament, God even sent enemy kings to fight wars against his own people, Israel, so that they would learn to think more about him and obey him all the time.

In the Bible God tells us that he sends troubles and trials into our lives for our good so that we may be better Christians. That means he disciplines us. Hebrews 12:10 says, "God disciplines us for our good, that we may share in his holiness." Let's learn that verse today.

I'll say the first part, and you say it after me. Then I'll say the rest, and you say that back to me just like an echo. After that we'll ask our moms and dads and everyone else to say it all together with us. Ready? "God disciplines us for our good" *(encourage children to echo phrase),* "that we may share in his holiness." *(Children echo.)* Hebrews 12, verse 10. *(Children echo.)* Now everyone. *(Lead all in saying verse and location.)*

If our parents correct us and discipline us when we do something wrong, we have to remember that they do this so we won't do that bad thing again. They want us to be the best boys or girls that we can be. God does the same thing to his children. He irons out our wrinkles. *(Hold up the handkerchiefs.)* When bad things happen to you, ask yourself, "What do you suppose God is trying to teach me now?" Then thank him for loving you.

Instead of Me

Concept: Jesus suffered the punishment for
   our sin.

Object: An old bird's nest or picture of one

Memory Verse: 1 John 3:16—This is how we
   know what love is: Jesus Christ laid down
   his life for us.

This morning I have something special to
show you. Can you tell me what this is? *(Hold up the
old bird's nest or picture of one. Allow responses.)* Good!
It sounds like you know quite a bit about birds' nests.
But tell me, why do birds build nests? *(Allow responses.)*
Yes, the mother bird needs a place to lay her eggs. After
awhile the eggs hatch and then both the father and
the mother birds bring food for the new little birds.

If a mother bird is sitting on the nest to keep the
eggs warm, the father bird often stays nearby. If a
person comes near the nest, the father bird may
think that person will harm the nest. He may chirp
loudly so the person will notice him instead of the
nest. He may land on the ground and act like he has
a broken wing. Then he may hop away from where
the nest is hidden. If the person begins to follow
him, he will hop a little farther away to lead the per-

son farther away from the nest. The father bird is trying to protect the mother bird and the eggs in the nest. He is risking his life to save the mother bird and the nest from harm. He would rather get caught than to have the person harm the nest.

Did you know that your parents would like to protect you that way too? If you are sick and need a shot, your mother may say, "Oh, I wish I could be sick instead of you," or "I know that shot will hurt, and I wish I could take the shot for you." The Bible tells us that Jesus loves us even more than that because he died on the cross for us so that we wouldn't have to be punished for our sins by going to hell. In 1 John 3:16 we read, "This is how we know what love is: Jesus Christ laid down his life for us." Let's learn that verse for our memory work today.

I'll say the first part, and you say it after me. Then I'll say the rest, and you say that back to me just like an echo. After that we'll ask our moms and dads and everyone else to say it all together with us. Ready? "This is how we know what love is" *(encourage children to echo phrase):* "Jesus Christ laid down his life for us." *(Children echo.)* First John 3, verse 16. *(Children echo.)* Now everyone. *(Lead all in saying verse and location.)*

Father and mother birds are willing to risk their lives for the eggs or the little birds in their nest. Our fathers and mothers would be willing to take our hurts instead of having us do so. But the greatest love in all the world is when our loving Savior went to the cross to suffer and die for our sins so we could go to heaven. Whenever you see a bird's nest *(hold it up),* remember to thank Jesus for his love for you.

Part **Three**

God's Care

God Cares for Us

Concept: God provides ways to protect us from harm.

Object: A child's car seat

Memory Verse: 1 Peter 5:7—Cast all your anxiety on him because he cares for you.

Do you know what this is? *(Show the car seat. Allow responses.)* Yes, you're right; it is a car seat. Today I want to talk a little bit about what car seats are for. First I want you to look at these straps. When somebody sits in the car seat, you have to have the straps tied. Otherwise sitting in the car seat wouldn't keep you from getting hurt if your car was in an accident.

There is one other important thing. The car seat needs to be fastened down carefully too. If a child was strapped into a car seat but the car seat wasn't fastened down well, it still wouldn't help to keep the child safe.

Sometimes little children don't like to be fastened in a car seat. They may even fuss or cry or stretch out so it is hard for their mother or dad to fasten the straps. Do you know why parents fasten the straps even though their children may not like it too well? *(Allow responses.)* Yes, parents want their children to be fastened safely in car seats or seat belts because they love their children and don't want them to get hurt in case of a car accident.

Our parents show they love us by taking good care of us. God loves us even more. He gives us car seats and seat belts so that parents can show their love for us by making us sit in them when we ride in a car.

There are lots of verses in the Bible that tell us that God cares for us. One is 1 Peter 5:7. It goes like this: "Cast all your anxiety on him because he cares for you." "Anxiety" means cares or worries.

I'll say the first part, and you say it after me. Then I'll say the rest, and you say that back to me just like an echo. After that we'll ask our moms and dads and everyone else to say it all together with us. Ready? "Cast all your anxiety on him" *(encourage children to echo phrase)* "because he cares for you." *(Children echo.)* First Peter 5, verse 7. *(Children echo.)* Now everyone. *(Lead all in saying verse and location.)*

I'm sure you have seen a little baby quietly sleeping in its mother's arms. The baby doesn't worry about anything. It trusts its mother to take care of it. That's what this verse tells us about how God is always caring for us. If you are learning to ride a bicycle and are afraid of falling, remember: "he cares for you." When you get older and fly in an airplane remember again: "he cares for you." Wherever you are, God's loving arms are always around you to care for you and keep you.

Each time you see a car seat *(hold up the seat)* or your parents ask you to buckle up in a seat belt, remember that your parents love and care for you. Remember especially that God loves and cares for you too.

11

God Sees What We Need

Concept: God sees us, knows us, and supplies our needs.

Objects: A fish in a fishbowl

Memory Verse: Matthew 6:8—Your Father knows what you need before you ask him.

Today, girls and boys, I brought along my special friend, (name of goldfish). *(Hold up your fishbowl so all the children can see the goldfish.)* Does anyone know why I didn't just bring him along in my pocket? *(Allow responses.)* Right. When God made the world he made fish too. And he planned that a fish needs to live in the water just like we need to live on land. So I keep (name of fish) in my fishbowl. I give him fresh water and I give him food when he needs it too.

I can watch (name of the fish) anytime I want to. All I have to do is look right through the glass. There's no place for (name of the fish) to hide. He can't even close his eyes and pretend to hide because fish don't have any eyelids. Anybody can see him anytime.

The Bible tells us that God sees us all the time. Sometimes when we do something that we know is wrong, we wish we could hide from God. But it doesn't matter if we are in the dark or the light, if we are nearby or far away, if we are inside a building or outside under the sky. God always sees us.

It's wonderful to have a God who always sees us because the God who always sees us loves us. He knows when we have problems. He knows when we're afraid. He can provide everything we need.

There's a verse in the Bible that we want to learn today. It's Matthew 6:8. It says, "Your Father knows what you need before you ask him."

I'll say the first part, and you say it after me. Then I'll say the rest, and you say that back to me just like an echo. After that we'll ask our moms and dads and everyone else to say it all together with us. Ready?

"Your Father knows what you need" *(encourage children to echo phrase)* "before you ask him." *(Children echo.)* Matthew 6, verse 8. *(Children echo.)* Now everyone. *(Lead all in saying verse and location.)*

Our heavenly Father sees us all the time *(hold up the fishbowl)* and knows everything we need even before we ask him. Let's remember that he always watches over us and cares for us.

12

All Things Work Together
for Our Good

Concept: God puts the many events in our lives together for our good.

Objects: Cake mix and ingredients to be added

Memory Verse: Romans 8:28—And we know that in all things God works for the good of those who love him.

Look at the picture on this box. *(Hold up box of cake mix.)* How many of you like to eat chocolate cake? *(Allow responses.)* Chocolate cake is really good, isn't it? One of the easiest ways to make a chocolate cake is to use a cake mix. You just open the box and eat it, right? *(Allow responses; then focus on a child who has given a negative response.)* Right! Just eating the dry, powdery flour out of the box wouldn't taste good at all. Here I have some other things to be added to the flour. I have an egg and some cooking oil. These wouldn't taste very good by themselves either. But when I mix all these things together and bake them in the oven, I have a delicious cake.

You already know that God watches over each one of us. He sends us times of happiness. He sends us times of sadness too. He sends us times when we feel really good. He sends us times when we are sick.

Our verse today tells us that everything that God sends us is for our good. You may ask, "How can this trouble be good for me?" The answer is that the time of trouble may not be very good by itself, but the verse says that all things work TOGETHER for our good. The oil by itself tastes terrible, but when it's mixed with all the other ingredients, it helps make a wonderful cake. Today's memory verse is Romans 8:28. It tells us the same thing. It says, "And we know that in all things God works for the good of those who love him."

I'll say the first part, and you say it after me. Then I'll say the rest, and you say that back to me just like an echo. After that we'll get our moms and dads and everyone else to say it all together with us. Ready? "And we know that in all things" *(encourage children to echo phrase)* "God works for the good of those who love him." *(Children echo.)* Romans 8, verse 28. *(Children echo.)* Now everyone. *(Lead all in saying verse and location.)*

In all the things that happen to us in our lives, God is working for our good. If we look at just one time of sickness or sorrow we might ask, "God, how is this good for me?" But God knows best. He puts all the good times and the bad times together *(hold up the mix and ingredients)* to make a plan for our lives that is best for us. *(Hold up the picture of the cake.)* Let's always remember that and thank him for his care.

13

Angels Are Always Watching

Concept: God places angels to watch over us all the time.

Object: Picture of a lifeguard

Memory Verse: Psalm 91:11—For he will command his angels concerning you to guard you in all your ways.

Today I have a picture I would like to show you. It's a picture of a lifeguard sitting on a chair on the beach. The chair is so high she has to climb a ladder to get up there. What does a lifeguard do up there on her chair? (Allow responses.) Right, she watches the swimmers in the water, and if she sees someone going out too far into the deep water, or who is calling for help, then what does she do? (Allow responses.) Yes, she saves them from drowning. Sometimes no lifeguard is on duty. Then there is a sign that says, Caution: No Lifeguard on Duty; Swim at Your Own Risk. That means that you have to be extra careful because there is no good swimmer watching over you. That's not a very safe feeling.

All through our lives people watch over us. Parents watch over us. Baby-sitters watch over us while our parents are away. Teachers watch over us in school. Policemen watch over us on the street.

But the Bible tells us about the most wonderful "watchers" of all. They are God's angels. In Psalm 91:11 we find this promise about God: "For he will command his angels concerning you to guard you in all your ways." Let's learn that verse today.

I'll say the first part, and you say it after me. Then I'll say the rest, and you say that back to me just like an echo. After that we'll ask our moms and dads and everyone else to say it all together with us. Ready? "For he will command his angels concerning you" *(encourage children to echo phrase)* "to guard you in all your ways." *(Children echo.)* Psalm 91, verse 11. *(Children echo.)* Now everyone. *(Lead all in saying verse and location.)*

God commands his angels to guard each of us. *(Hold up the picture.)* It's hard to imagine, isn't it? Think of how many angels there must be. The Bible says there are hosts of angels. That means there are lots and lots of them, so they can easily do what God tells them to do. Because we can't see angels, we sometimes forget that they are always near us. But they are. Let's be sure to thank God for sending his angels to guard and protect us.

Find a Safe Place

Concept: In times of danger and trouble God is our refuge.

Object: Picture of an area destroyed by a tornado or earthquake

Memory Verse: Psalm 46:1—God is our refuge and strength, an ever-present help in trouble.

If there was a tornado coming, all the sirens would be blowing and we would have to stay home from church, wouldn't we? A tornado has very strong winds that can blow trees down. A tornado can even blow roofs off houses. Look at this picture I brought today. *(Hold up the picture.)* Can you see what happened when the storm came? *(Allow responses.)* Yes, the tornado really did a lot of damage. Sometimes people get hurt in storms like this. What should you do if you hear a tornado warning or even a severe thunderstorm warning? *(Allow responses.)* Right; you need to go to a safe place. A safe place is often called a shelter or a refuge. That means you have to go to a corner of the basement or another place in your house that is extra strong.

King David was a warrior in Bible times who had many enemies. Sometimes he would hide in caves to escape from those who wanted to kill him. Later on in his life he wrote the Book of Psalms. In Psalm 46:1 he wrote about the best refuge of all. He wrote this: "God is our refuge and strength, an ever-present help in trouble." That's still as true for us as it was for David. Let's learn that verse today.

I'll say the first part, and you say it after me. Then I'll say the rest, and you say that back to me just like an echo. After that we'll ask our moms and dads and everyone else to say it all together with us. Ready? "God is our refuge and strength" *(encourage children to echo phrase),* "an ever-present help in trouble." *(Children echo.)* Psalm 46, verse 1. *(Children echo.)* Now everyone. *(Lead all in saying verse and location.)*

In many places the Bible tells us about how strong God is. He can stop a storm. He can divide the sea so his people can cross on dry land. He can make the forests grow and can bring rain for the crops. He can carry us carefully in his arms.

When a real storm or earthquake comes *(hold up the picture),* we usually don't have a lot of time to decide where we need to go to be safe. The best thing to do is to pick out the safest spot to be before the storm or earthquake comes. That's why schools have fire drills. Some places even have tornado and earthquake drills. They do this so everyone will know exactly what to do in an emergency. Some public buildings even have signs pointing to shelter areas so people will quickly be able to find the safest place to go. We need to plan ahead too. We need to pray to God every day to ask for his care. We always need to make him our strength and refuge. Then in an emergency, we'll know we can come to God. We'll know that he is our ever-present help in trouble. Don't just go to God in times of trouble; make him your friend every day!

Part Four

God's Promises

15

Trust Me

Concept: Depend on God's wisdom, not your own.

Object: Pair of crutches

Memory Verse: Proverbs 3:5—Trust in the LORD with all your heart and lean not on your own understanding; in all your ways acknowledge him, and he will make your paths straight.

Girls and boys, do you know what these are? *(Show them the crutches. Allow responses.)* Good. Do you know why people use crutches? *(Allow responses.)* Right! If you have a broken bone in your leg or ankle, you don't want to use that leg or ankle because it isn't strong enough to hold you up. You need to lean on crutches like these. Leaning on something else is very important if you can't stand up by yourself. When you use crutches you have to trust that they will be strong enough to hold you up.

The Bible talks about leaning too. In Proverbs 3:5 it tells us not to lean on ourselves and our own wisdom because we are not strong enough and wise enough without God. It says, "Trust in the LORD with all your heart and lean not on your own understanding; in all your ways acknowledge him, and he will make your paths straight." Let's learn that verse today.

I'll say the first part, and you say it after me. Then I'll say the rest, and you say that back to me just like an echo. After that we'll ask our moms and dads and everyone else to say it all together with us. Ready? "Trust in the LORD with all your heart and lean not on your own understanding" *(encourage children to echo phrase);* "in all your ways acknowledge him" *(children echo),* "and he will make your paths straight." *(Children echo.)* Proverbs 3, verse 5. *(Children echo.)* Now everyone. *(Lead all in saying verse and location.)*

It's good to have crutches to lean on; they hold you up when you have a broken leg. *(Hold up crutches.)* It's much better to have a wise and loving God whom we can always lean on for wisdom. We must not think we're so smart we don't need God. If we tried to run our lives without God we would soon be on the wrong path. But if we lean on God's wisdom, we know that God will always direct us in the right way to go.

16

God Watches Over You While You Sleep

Concept: Even while we sleep God watches over us.

Object: Pillow

Memory Verse: Psalm 121:3–4—He who watches over you will not slumber; indeed, he who watches over Israel will neither slumber nor sleep.

This is my favorite pillow, girls and boys. *(Hold up the pillow.)* It's nice and soft, and it feels so good when I hug it close to me. Do you have a favorite pillow too? *(Allow responses.)* When is the best time to use a pillow? *(Allow responses.)* Yes, we use a pillow most often when we sleep. And we do sleep quite a lot, don't we? Little tiny babies sleep almost half of every day. Then they sleep most of the night too.

When babies get a little older, they just take naps in the afternoon. Older children like you don't need to nap during the day anymore. You can just sleep on your pillow at night. *(Hold up the pillow.)*

Sometimes people are afraid during the night. They may just be afraid because it's so dark. Or they may hear some scary noises and wonder what they are.

There is one thing all of us can do if we are afraid in the nighttime. We can pray to Jesus to keep us safe while we are asleep. If you don't know how to pray at bedtime, just ask your mom or dad to help you.

One other thing to remember if you wake up or can't get to sleep because you are afraid is that Jesus is always awake. He can see you and watch over you even in the darkest night. How can we be sure that he will? The Bible tells us so! The memory verse we have today will help us remember that God always watches over us. It is Psalm 121:3–4. It says, "He who watches over you will not slumber; indeed, he who watches over Israel will neither slumber nor sleep."

I'll say the first part, and you say it after me. Then I'll say the rest, and you say that back to me just like an echo. After that we'll ask your moms and dads and everyone else to say it all together with us. Ready? "He who watches over you will not slumber" *(encourage children to echo phrase);* "indeed, he who watches over Israel will neither slumber nor sleep." *(Children echo.)* Psalm 121, verses 3 and 4. *(Children echo.)* Now everyone. *(Lead all in saying verse and location.)*

Even during the darkest night, God watches over us, and he never sleeps. The next time you are alone in the dark, just lie back on your nice, soft pillow *(hold the pillow to the side of your head)* and remember that you are safe even while you sleep because God is always watching over and guarding you.

17

Jesus Died to Save Sinners

Concept: Because God loved the world, he
   sent Jesus to save sinners.

Object: A life jacket

Memory Verse: John 3:16—For God so loved
   the world that he gave his one and only
   Son, that whoever believes in him shall not
   perish but have eternal life.

Now many of you like to go swimming?
(Allow responses.) Why is trying to swim in deep water
sometimes dangerous? *(Allow responses.)* Yes, swimming in deep water or when there are big waves can
be very dangerous even if a person is a very good
swimmer.

When people take their boats out into deep water
it's very important to wear a life jacket. *(Put yours on
to demonstrate.)* I don't know exactly what a life
jacket is made of, but it must have some material in
it that is very light, because it floats. In fact, if the
person wearing this life jacket would fall off a boat
into deep water, the life jacket would keep that person from drowning. If a big ship starts to sink out
in the ocean, the passengers quickly put on life jack-
ets and get into lifeboats to keep them from perish-

ing, or dying, in the water. If they didn't do that, they would surely drown.

The Bible tells us that all people are sinners and that they will perish unless they are saved. The way to be saved is to believe in Jesus. He is the only one who can save people from their sins. That sounds simple, doesn't it? Well, it is. Just like putting on this life jacket. It isn't hard at all, but if I'm on a sinking boat out in the ocean, I'll drown unless I'm willing to put my life jacket on.

Our verse today is John 3:16. It says, "For God so loved the world that he gave his one and only Son, that whoever believes in him shall not perish but have eternal life." Let's learn that verse today.

I'll say the first part, and you say it after me. Then I'll say another part, and you say that back to me just like an echo. After that we'll ask our moms and dads and everyone else to say it all together with us. Ready? "For God so loved the world that he gave his one and only Son" *(encourage children to echo phrase),* "that whoever believes in him shall not perish but have eternal life." *(Children echo.)* John 3, verse 16. *(Children echo.)* Now everyone. *(Lead all in saying verse and location.)*

A life jacket is a lifesaver. If you simply put it on and fasten the ties so it stays around you *(demonstrate),* it can save you from drowning. It doesn't help a bit, however, if you're sinking in deep water and your life jacket is on the dock. Salvation is something like that. If you believe in Jesus and accept him as your Savior, God promises you eternal life. Be sure you believe in Jesus as your Savior today; tomorrow may be too late.

18

Waiting for a Call

Concept: God promises to answer our prayers.

Object: Telephone

Memory Verse: Isaiah 65:24—Before they call I will answer; while they are still speaking I will hear.

All of you know what this is *(hold up the telephone)*, don't you? *(Allow responses.)* Yes, it's a telephone. A telephone is a wonderful invention. Someone from far away can make a call and the phone in your house rings. Then you can talk to the person who called. What are some of the things you have to remember if you answer the phone? *(Allow responses.)* Yes, there are lots of things to remember so that you answer the phone correctly.

Sometimes your mom or dad or someone in your family may be expecting an important call. Maybe your grandma isn't feeling well and your parents are waiting for a call from someone to tell them how she is getting along.

When we expect special calls we usually stay near the telephone so that if it does ring, we can quickly answer it. We hardly even let the phone ring more than once because we can't wait to get the news.

When we pray to our heavenly Father, it's something like making a telephone call from earth to heaven except that we don't need phones like this *(hold yours up)*. We don't need telephone wires or telephone poles. We can just talk to God from wherever we are. The Bible tells us that he will hear and answer our prayers. In fact, Isaiah 65:24 tells us that God is so eager to hear from his children that he answers us even before we call. That's a promise we're going to learn for our memory verse today. "Before they call I will answer; while they are still speaking I will hear."

I'll say the first part, and you say it after me. Then I'll say the rest, and you say that back to me just like an echo. After that we'll ask our moms and dads and everyone else to say it all together with us. Ready? "Before they call I will answer" *(encourage children to echo phrase);* "while they are still speaking I will hear." *(Children echo.)* Isaiah 65, verse 24. *(Children echo.)* Now everyone. *(Lead all in saying verse and location.)*

Sometimes when we pray, we wonder if God wants to be bothered with the things we want to talk to him about. We shouldn't feel that way, because just like we are sometimes anxious to get a call from a friend or some member of the family *(hold up the telephone),* so God is eager to hear from each of his children. The Bible tells us that God is so ready to answer our prayers, he has the answer all ready even before we call. Let's pray to him often.

19

Nothing Can Separate Us from God's Love

Concept: God's love is always near us.

Objects: Pictures of various fences

Memory Verse: Romans 8:39—Neither height nor depth, nor anything else in all creation, will be able to separate us from the love of God.

Let's imagine, girls and boys, that you have a new puppy and the puppy is just about old enough to be away from its mother. Then you try to separate them. One way to do that is to put the puppy in a fenced-in part of the backyard. *(Hold up various pictures.)* How do you suppose the puppy would try to get out? *(Allow responses.)* Right. So to keep him from jumping over it you would need quite a high fence like this one. *(Show a picture of a high fence.)* What else could the puppy do? *(Allow responses.)* Right again. He might try to dig a hole underneath. So to keep the puppy separated from its mother and inside the fence, you would have to plan for that when you built the fence. You would have to dig a trench and put the boards or the wire down into the ground deep enough so the puppy couldn't dig under it to get out.

One place where we see very high, strong fences is around the prisons of our country. Persons who have done very bad things are sent to these prisons to keep them separate from the rest of the people. Here's a picture of a fence around a prison. *(Show the picture.)* Look at how high it is. It even has barbed wire with sharp points all along the top. It wouldn't be very nice to be locked inside a fence like that.

There are many ways to separate people from people. Long ago Christians were locked into prisons. They were put on lonely islands. They were even put in deep dungeons. Even today, people can be punished by being put in isolation, that is, they are kept separate from everyone else.

But there's no way we can be separated from God's love. God promises in Romans 8:39, "Neither height nor depth, nor anything else in all creation, will be able to separate us from the love of God." Let's learn that verse today.

I'll say the first part, and you say it after me. Then I'll say the rest, and you say that back to me just like an echo. After that we'll ask our moms and dads and everyone else to say it all together with us. Ready? "Neither height nor depth, nor anything else in all creation" *(encourage children to echo phrase),* "will be able to separate us from the love of God." *(Children echo.)* Romans 8, verse 39. *(Children echo.)* Now everyone. *(Lead all in saying verse and location.)*

God promises that his love is always all around us and nothing, not the highest fence *(hold up fence pictures),* the deepest dungeon, or anything else in all the world, can keep God's love away from us.

Part Five
God's Family

20

The Body of Christ Has Many Members

Concept: Each member of the church is important.

Objects: A model car with some removable parts

Memory Verse: 1 Corinthians 12:27—Now you are the body of Christ, and each one of you is a part of it.

Today I brought a model with me. *(Hold up the car.)* Can you tell me what this is a model of? *(Allow responses.)* Yes, it's a model of a _____ (name of the type of car). Now I'll take off a part. *(Take off a wheel and hold it up.)* Can you tell me what this is? *(Allow responses.)* Right! It is a wheel. A wheel isn't the whole car, but it is a very important part of the car. The car wouldn't be able to go very far without it. Even though the wheel is an important part of the car, there are lots of other important parts too. Can you name some of them? *(Allow responses.)* Yes, a car needs all of those parts and many more too. Did you know that in some ways our church is like a car? Our church, the body of Christ, has many members just as the car has many parts. The Bible tells us that every member of the church is important to all the rest.

In the church in Corinth long ago some of the people thought they were much more important than others. Then the apostle Paul wrote a letter to them to help them understand what the church was like. That letter is now part of the Bible. In his letter Paul said the church was like a body made up of many parts. The body needs feet; the body needs hands; the body needs ears and eyes. Then he wrote the words of today's memory verse. It's 1 Corinthians 12:27. It says, "Now you are the body of Christ, and each one of you is a part of it." Let's learn that verse today.

I'll say the first part, and you say it after me. Then I'll say the rest, and you say that back to me just like an echo. After that we'll ask our moms and dads and everyone else to say it all together with us. Ready? "Now you are the body of Christ" *(encourage children to echo phrase),* "and each one of you is a part of it." *(Children echo.)* First Corinthians 12, verse 27. *(Children echo.)* Now everyone. *(Lead all in saying verse and location.)*

Whenever you look at a model car *(hold up yours),* or whenever you look at a regular, full-sized one, remember that it takes lots and lots of different parts to make the car run well. Even the tiny little parts are needed. Then remember that the church is like that too. Every member is an important part of it. Every member is needed. Be sure to do your part to make it work well.

21

Reflecting God's Holiness

Concept: God commands us to be holy as he is holy.

Object: A mirror

Memory Verse: Leviticus 19:1—Be holy because I, the LORD your God, am holy.

If you look at me, you can see what I look like. You see that I have (color) hair. I (wear/don't wear) glasses. *(Continue in similar fashion.)* You can tell what I look like just by looking at me. How can you tell what you look like? *(Allow responses.)* Right. You could look at a picture of yourself or you could look in a mirror. *(Hold up the mirror so they can see themselves.)* Sometimes when a family has its picture taken, you can also see ways that you look like your parents or grandparents. Someone might look at your family picture and say, "You can see that (child's name) looks just like her mother," or, "It looks like (child's name) will be tall just like his dad."

It's wonderful to be part of a family here on earth, but it's even more wonderful to be part of God's family. Did you know that the Bible expects all God's children to be like their heavenly Father?

When people see you, they can see that you look like other members of your family. But people notice more than how you look. They also notice how you act. They listen to what you say.

To show others that we are part of the family of God we need to act like Christians. We need to act like children of our heavenly Father. He is perfect. That means he is holy. The Bible tells us to be that way too. In Leviticus 10:1 we read, "Be holy because I, the LORD your God, am holy." Let's learn that verse today to help us try to be like him.

I'll say it, and then you say it back to me just like an echo. After that we'll ask our moms and dads and everyone else to say it all together with us. Ready? "Be holy because I, the LORD your God, am holy." *(Encourage children to say verse.)* Leviticus 19, verse 1. *(Children echo.)* Now everyone. *(Lead all in saying verse and location.)*

Did you ever try to follow your mom or dad when they were walking in the snow or in the sand? They take such big steps. You can hardly stretch your legs far enough to walk in their footsteps. That's what it's like to try to be as holy and perfect as God is. He is without sin. He wants his children to grow up to be like he is. You don't need a mirror to see what God wants you to look like. *(Hold up mirror.)* Instead you just need the Bible. It will tell you how God wants you to live. Then people who look at you will know you are really members of God's family.

22

Christians Are Eager to Spend Time with God

> **Concept:** Christians should be as eager to spend time with God as a thirsty animal is to have a drink.
>
> **Object:** Picture of a deer or a mounted deer head
>
> **Memory Verse:** Psalm 42:1–2—As the deer pants for streams of water, so my soul pants for you, O God. My soul thirsts for God, for the living God.

How many of you have seen a dog hold its tongue out and pant during hot weather to cool itself off? *(Allow responses.)* Good. Any animal that has a coat of fur may get very warm when the weather gets hot. Then a dog or even a deer *(hold up your picture or mounted deer head)* needs to cool off. One way for an animal to do this is to open its mouth, put its tongue out, and pant so that it can take in lots of cool air. What else could the deer do to cool off? *(Allow responses.)* Yes, it could take a drink of cool water, and if we have a really hot day, we have to be sure that our pets also have enough cool water to drink.

When the pioneers came west across the prairie they would sometimes have to travel a long time without water. The animals as well as the people would get very thirsty. Then if the animals smelled a stream of water, even before they could see it, they would walk faster and even run toward it for a drink.

Long ago when King David was still a young boy, he tended his father's sheep. He probably saw deer and even hunted them for food. He knew that if a hunter was chasing a deer, the deer would run and run to get away. Then the deer would get very hot and thirsty and would try to find a stream of water so it could get a refreshing drink.

Later on in his life, David wrote many psalms. He wrote Psalm 42 when he thought about a deer that was very thirsty for a drink of water. It reminded him of how much he wanted to spend time with God. It says, "As the deer pants for streams of water, so my soul pants for you, O God. My soul thirsts for God, for the living God." These verses are our memory work for today.

I'll say the first part, and you say it after me. Then I'll say the next part, and you say it after me. Then I'll say the rest, and you say that back to me just like an echo. After that we'll ask our moms and dads and everyone else to say it all together with us. Ready? "As the deer pants for streams of water" *(encourage children to echo phrase)*, "so my soul pants for you, O God." *(Children echo.)* "My soul thirsts for God, for the living God." *(Children echo.)* Psalm 42, verses 1 and 2. *(Children echo.)* Now everyone. *(Lead all in saying verse and location.)*

If the members of God's family really love him, they will want to spend a lot of time with him. You as a member of God's family will want to pray to him and you will want to read his holy Word, the Bible. You will be as anxious to be with God as a thirsty animal is to find a drink of water. *(Hold up the picture or head.)* Whenever you see an animal that is thirsty and give it a drink of water, remember how anxious David was to be with God. Then remember how nice it is for you to spend time with God.

23

God's Family Shares

Concept: Christians show their love by doing good things for one another.

Objects: Scissors, pan of water, towel

Memory Verse: Galatians 6:10—As we have opportunity, let us do good to all people, especially to those who belong to the family of believers.

Today we want to think about how important it is for Christians to help one another. First I'd like to have you look at these scissors. *(Hold them up.)* Can you tell me how many parts they have? *(Allow responses.)* Yes, two parts. Can you see how the two parts are fastened together in the middle? *(Allow responses.)* What would happen if these scissors only had one part? *(Allow responses.)* Right; one part just couldn't cut by itself. It couldn't do what it's supposed to do without the other part.

Now I'd like you to watch me wash my hands in this pan of water. First I'll wash one hand and dry it on a towel. *(Do so, keeping the other hand behind your back.)* Well, this doesn't work very well, does it? Do any of you know what I could do instead of washing and drying one hand at a time? *(Allow responses.)*

Right! One hand could help the other one. It's just like trying to clap with only one hand. *(Demonstrate or have children try.)* If hands clap together it works better.

The Bible says Christians should help each other. In Galatians 6:10 we read, "As we have opportunity, let us do good to all people, especially to those who belong to the family of believers." Let's learn that verse today.

I'll say the first part, and you say it after me. Then I'll say the rest, and you say that back to me just like an echo. After that we'll ask our moms and dads and everyone else to say it all together with us. Ready? "As we have opportunity, let us do good to all people" *(encourage children to echo phrase)*, "especially to those who belong to the family of believers." *(Children echo.)* Galatians 6, verse 10. *(Children echo.)* Now everyone. *(Lead all in saying verse and location.)*

It's true that good things happen when people help each other. *(Demonstrate working scissors.)* Doing good things for others is an important part of being a Christian. The Bible says we need to look for ways to do good to others. The Bible also says that we have to be extra careful to help Christians who are in need. That's an important way to show our love for Jesus, who is the head of the family of God.

Don't Be Ashamed of Jesus

Concept: We should not be ashamed to tell others we are Christians.

Objects: Bulletin cover or church stationery, picture of a cross, and a picture of a fish as a Christian symbol

Memory Verse: 1 Peter 4:16—If you suffer as a Christian, do not be ashamed, but praise God that you bear that name.

I'm sure glad to see you in church today, boys and girls. Our church has a name. Do you know what it is? *(Allow responses.)* Right! *(Repeat the name with emphasis on the word "church" and also the word "Christian" if it is in the name of your church.)* I brought with me some of the paper the secretary uses when she writes letters from the church. *(Hold it up.)* If you look at it carefully you will see the word "church" just as it is on the sign in front of the church building.

Many churches have a cross like this *(show them the cross or picture of one that you brought)* on the steeple or inside the building. Do you know why many churches have a cross outside or inside? *(Allow responses.)* Yes, because Christ Jesus died on a cross.

Because we go to church and believe in Christ we are called Christians. Long ago when the followers of Christ first began meeting together, people who did not love Jesus poked fun of the people who did. They called those who followed Christ, "Christians."

Today there are still many people who do not love Jesus. Many of them still like to make fun of those who do. The Bible tells us in 1 Peter 4:16 that we should not be ashamed if we have to suffer for being a Christian. Instead we should be glad and praise God when people make fun of us for being like Christ Jesus. Let's learn that important verse today.

I'll say the first part and you say it after me. Then I'll say the rest, and you say that back to me just like an echo. After that we'll ask our moms and dads and everyone else to say it all together with us. Ready? "If you suffer as a Christian, do not be ashamed" *(encourage children to echo phrase),* "but praise God that you bear that name." *(Children echo.)* First Peter 4, verse 16. *(Children echo.)* Now everyone. *(Lead all in saying the verse and location.)*

You know how people act when they are ashamed of something. They try to hide what they are ashamed of. Long ago Nicodemus came to Jesus by night because he didn't want others to know that he was a follower of Jesus. Peter was ashamed of Jesus on the night Jesus was crucified, so he said he never even knew who Jesus was. Some people are afraid to pray in a restaurant because they think others would know they are Christians.

Are you afraid to let others know that you are a Christian? Maybe you can let others know by wearing a small cross. Some people put a symbol like this *(hold up the symbol of the fish)* on their cars to let others know they are Christians. Best of all, live like Jesus wants you to live. Never be ashamed of being a Christian. Instead be thankful that you can be called by that name!

Part Six

The *I Am's* of Jesus

25

"I Am the Bread of Life"

Concept: Just as we depend on bread for food for our bodies, so we must look to Jesus for food for our souls.

Objects: A loaf of bread, a Bible

Memory Verse: John 6:35—Jesus declared, "I am the bread of life. He who comes to me will never go hungry."

I'm sure all of you girls and boys know what this is. *(Hold up the loaf of bread.)* Right! It's a loaf of white bread. How many other kinds of bread can you think of? *(Allow responses.)* Good! You already know there are many different kinds of bread, and I'm sure that if you went to a bakery or grocery store to buy a loaf of bread you would find many more kinds to choose from: regular loaves, short loaves, long loaves, round loaves, square loaves. Loaves of bread can be made in lots of different shapes and sizes.

People in different parts of the world have many different kinds of food, but the one food that is found almost everywhere is bread. *(Hold up your loaf.)* Sometimes we bake bread in our ovens at home. Some people have bread machines that bake one loaf at a time. Bakeries bake many loaves of bread at once in big ovens. Some people bake their bread over an open fire or in brick ovens.

Sometimes we have so much to eat that we like pudding or pie or ice cream for dessert after a meal better than bread. But if people are very, very hungry or if they have very little food, they don't worry about dessert. They just wish they had bread to eat. They don't worry about whether it has jelly or peanut butter on it, they just wish they had some bread to keep them alive.

Just as bread like this *(hold up loaf)* is needed to keep our bodies alive, so we need Jesus to give life to our souls. We need to learn more about Jesus from the Bible *(hold up Bible)* every day as much as we need food for our bodies. Let's use our verse today to help us remember that by believing in Jesus we have life for our souls. The verse is John 6:35. It says, "Jesus declared, 'I am the bread of life. He who comes to me will never go hungry.'"

I'll say the first part, and you say it after me. Then I'll say the rest, and you say that back to me just like an echo. After that we'll ask our moms and dads and everyone else to say it all together with us. Ready? "Jesus declared, 'I am the bread of life'" *(encourage children to echo phrase).* "'He who comes to me will never go hungry.'" *(Children echo.)* John 6, verse 35. *(Children echo.)* Now everyone. *(Lead all in saying verse and location.)*

When we get hungry for food and enjoy the bread that God gives us to keep our bodies alive, let's not forget that it is Jesus who keeps our souls alive. He feeds our souls with spiritual food each time we read the Bible. He is our bread of life.

26

Jesus—the Source of Living Water

Concept: If we drink regular water we will get thirsty again, but Jesus' water keeps us alive forever.

Objects: Two potted plants, one living, the other withered and obviously dead

Memory Verse: John 4:13—Jesus answered, "Everyone who drinks this water will be thirsty again, but whoever drinks the water I give him will never thirst."

Today I brought two plants with me. *(Hold them up.)* Can anyone tell me why they look different? *(Allow responses.)* That's right; the one in this pot has nice green leaves and the other has lost all its leaves and doesn't look good at all. Why do you think one is alive and the other is dead? *(Allow responses.)* Yes, I'm afraid that's what happened. When I watered my plants, I missed giving this one any water. Its leaves started to wither away and drop off. If I had noticed it in time, I probably could have saved it, but now it's too late. The plant is dead.

Water is necessary for people just as it is necessary for plants. If we don't get any water to drink, we get

70

very thirsty. If a person gets lost in the desert and can't get any water at all, that person will die.

When Jesus was sitting by a well in Samaria one day, a woman came to the well to get water. Jesus wanted her to know how very important it was to have eternal life. He told her he was the only one who could give her "living" water. This is how Jesus taught her that he was the Savior. The Bible tells us in John 4:13 that "Jesus answered, 'Everyone who drinks this water will be thirsty again, but whoever drinks the water I give him will never thirst.'" Let's learn that verse today.

I'll say the first part, and you say it after me. Then I'll say the rest, and you say that back to me just like an echo. After that we'll get our moms and dads and everyone else to say it all together with us. Ready? "Jesus answered, 'Everyone who drinks this water will be thirsty again'" *(encourage children to echo phrase)*, "'but whoever drinks the water I give him will never thirst.'" *(Children echo.)* John 4, verse 13. *(Children echo.)* Now everyone. *(Lead all in saying verse and location.)*

Without water a plant like this one *(hold up the dead plant)* just withers away and dies. Our verse today tells us that if we are to live forever, we need living water. We need Jesus. We can't live without him. Let's remember that every time we water our plants.

27

"I Am the Good Shepherd"

Concept: Jesus cares for us as a shepherd cares for sheep.

Objects: Picture of a shepherd and sheep, a piece of woolly sheepskin

Memory Verse: John 10:14—I am the good shepherd; I know my sheep and my sheep know me.

How many of you girls and boys have touched a sheep's wool? *(Allow responses.)* Good. If you haven't felt wool before, I would like to have you feel how nice and soft this is. *(Let them feel the sheepskin.)* Now let's look at this picture of a shepherd and his sheep. *(Hold up picture.)* What does the shepherd do to take care of his sheep? *(Allow responses.)* Yes, those are things a shepherd does. The shepherd takes the sheep to a quiet stream to drink. The shepherd takes them to a pasture where there are no poisonous weeds or dangerous rocks. The shepherd also protects them from wolves or other animals that would harm them.

Sheep and little lambs are really nice animals, but they aren't very smart. Did you know that in our country over one thousand sheep die every year

72

because they turn over on their backs when they lie down and can't get up again? Sheep stray away and get lost and can't find their way back. No, sheep aren't very smart; in fact, they're kind of stupid. But did you know that the Bible says people are like sheep? We sometimes eat the wrong kind of food. We get lost and go to the wrong places. We need a shepherd to keep us safe. Jesus tells us in John 10:14 that he is our Shepherd. He said, "I am the good shepherd; I know my sheep and my sheep know me." Let's learn that verse today.

I'll say the first part, and you say it after me. Then I'll say the rest, and you say that back to me just like an echo. After that we'll ask our moms and dads and everyone else to say it all together with us. Ready? "I am the good shepherd" *(encourage children to echo phrase);* "I know my sheep and my sheep know me." *(Children echo.)* John 10, verse 14. *(Children echo.)* Now everyone. *(Lead all in saying verse and location.)*

Jesus truly is a good shepherd. He knows us all by name. He is with us always to watch over us and care for us. He died to save us from our sins. If we get lost, he comes to find us and bring us back to him again. What a wonderful Shepherd we have! We must always follow him!

28

"I Am the Vine; You Are the Branches"

Concept: To be spiritually alive, you must be joined to Jesus Christ.

Object: A branch recently cut off a tree

Memory Verse: John 15:5—I am the vine; you are the branches.

Today I brought with me a branch (or stem from a plant) that I just cut off the tree yesterday. *(Hold up the branch or stem.)* What is beginning to happen to the leaves? *(Allow responses.)* Yes, the leaves are starting to wilt. They look all bent over and saggy, don't they? Why do you suppose they look like this? *(Allow responses.)* Right. Because the branch is cut off the tree, the leaves can't get any more water or food from the root of the tree. What do you think is going to happen to this branch and all the leaves on it? *(Allow responses.)* That's right. Because the branch is no longer fastened to the tree, it will slowly die. First the leaves will dry up and fall off, and then slowly the branch will turn brown and hard.

When Jesus was on earth, he used a vine with its branches to teach us an important lesson. He said that he was like a vine that sends life-giving water and food to us, the branches. Then Jesus told his followers that unless they stayed connected to him they couldn't bear fruit. In fact, he said, "Apart from me you can do nothing." In John 15:5 Jesus said, "I am the vine; you are the branches." Let's learn those words as our memory work for today.

I'll say it and you say it after me just like an echo. After that we'll ask our moms and dads and everyone else to say it all together with us. Ready? "I am the vine; you are the branches." *(Encourage children to say verse.)* John 15, verse 5. *(Children echo.)* Now everyone. *(Lead all in saying verse and location.)*

If you cut a stem or branch from a living plant or tree the stem or branch soon dies. *(Hold up branch.)* How important it is for all Christians to stay in touch with Christ. It's the only way to stay spiritually alive, to learn more about how Jesus wants us to live, and to get the strength from him to do so every day. How can you stay closely connected to Jesus? One way is to pray every day. Another way is to listen to Bible stories to learn more about Jesus. But the best way to stay connected to him is to live the way he wants you to live and do the things he wants you to do. Then you will be a living branch connected to Jesus.

29

"I Am the Light of the World"

> **Concept:** Those who follow Jesus walk in his light.
>
> **Objects:** Several types of night-lights, a candle
>
> **Memory Verse:** John 8:12—I am the light of the world. Whoever follows me will never walk in darkness.

Some of you girls and boys may have been in a really, really dark place. If all the lights in your house are shut off at night, it may seem quite dark, but usually a little light comes in from a streetlight or a yard light. You may even get some light from the moon or the stars. If it's really dark in your house at night, what could you do? *(Allow responses.)* Right! Look at some of the different kinds of night-lights I have. The first one is a candle. *(Hold up the candle.)* People used to use candles a lot before we had electricity to light our homes. We have to be very careful with candles. Do you know why? *(Allow responses.)* Yes, a candle flame can give light but it can start a fire too. We have to be very careful not to set candles too close to something that could catch fire. We have to remember to blow them out when we are through with them. But now let me show you some

76

of the other kinds of night-lights that I found. *(Hold them up.)* They all look different, but they all help us by giving us light.

Do you know of someplace that's really dark? *(Allow responses.)* Yes, all those places could be really dark. Someday you may go on a trip to visit some of our national parks. In one of these parks there is a cave that goes deep down into the earth. Then when all the visitors are down there, the park ranger tells everyone that he is going to turn off the lights for a little while so the visitors can find out what it's like to be in absolute darkness. It's scary. Everyone feels better when he turns the lights on again and even better when they get out of the cave in the sunlight once more.

Sin is something like darkness. It keeps people from doing the right things and staying on the right path following Jesus. The devil wants us to do bad things. The Bible tells us that Satan is the ruler of the kingdom of darkness and he tries to lead us the wrong way to do things that God doesn't want us to do. That's why Jesus said in John 8:12, "I am the light of the world. Whoever follows me will never walk in darkness." Let's learn that wonderful verse about Jesus today.

I'll say the first part, and you say it after me. Then I'll say the rest, and you say that back to me just like an echo. After that we'll ask our moms and dads and everyone else to say it all together with us. Ready? "I am the light of the world" *(encourage children to echo phrase)*. "Whoever follows me will never walk in darkness."*(Children echo.)* John 8, verse 12. *(Children echo.)* Now everyone. *(Lead all in saying verse and location.)*

If we stumble around away from Jesus in the darkness of sin, we may lose our way. We may follow wrong people who think they know the right path. Doing that could end up being very dangerous. Follow Jesus, who is the light of the world. Do what he wants you to do and go where he wants you to go. Then you'll be on God's path.

Part Seven

Living for Jesus

30

Be Sure to Start at the Right Place

> **Concept:** To end at the right place, you need to start at the right place.
>
> **Object:** Sweater or coat that fastens with buttons
>
> **Memory Verse:** Psalm 111:10—The fear of the LORD is the beginning of wisdom.

How many of you have a sweater or coat that you have to close with a zipper? *(Allow responses.)* Well, I wore my sweater (or coat) today and it doesn't have a zipper. To close this sweater (or coat), you have to button the buttons. Buttoning buttons can be quite a job. But just watch me, and I'll show you how to do it. *(Demonstrate buttoning up your sweater or coat, but put the first button in a buttonhole that is one space too high. Begin speaking when you get to the last button.)* Uh-oh; look what happened. It's not even. What do you think is wrong? *(Allow responses.)* Yes, I guess I'll just have to unbutton it and start over. *(Unbutton and try again. This time make the other side come out too long.)* There. I did it over. Is it right now? *(Allow responses.)* Uh-oh; I must have made a mistake. Now this side is too short. I must have started at the wrong place again. I better unbutton it and try again. *(Unbutton.)* This time, first I'm going to look at the bottom and make the ends even, and then I'll match up the sides so I'll be sure to start at the right place. *(Do so.)* Now it should come out just right. Let's see if it does. Yes, now it's even. I must have started at the right place.

Beginning at the right place is really important when you try to button a sweater (or coat), isn't it? There is a verse in the Bible that talks about beginning at the right place. It's Psalm 111:10. It says, "The fear of the LORD is the beginning of wisdom." Let's learn that verse today.

I'll say the first part, and you say it after me. Then I'll say the rest, and you say that back to me just like an echo. After that we'll ask our moms and dads and everyone else to say it all together with us. Ready? "The fear of the LORD" *(encourage children to echo phrase)* "is the beginning of wisdom." *(Children echo.)* Psalm 111, verse 10. *(Children echo.)* Now everyone. *(Lead all in saying verse and location.)*

Remember that when you button your sweater or coat, you need to begin at the right place if you want to end up at the right place. *(Point to your sweater or coat.)* Our lives and all the things we do are like that too. If you want to end at the right place, you have to start at the right place. If we want to end with wisdom, we need to begin with God.

31

Love Builds Strong and Happy Christians

Concept: When Christians love one another they help build happy, strong families and churches.

Object: A set of building blocks

Memory Verse: John 15:12—Love each other as I have loved you.

I'm sure that many of you have tried to make a high tower with building blocks, haven't you? *(Show the blocks.)* What's the first thing you have to do? *(Allow responses.)* Right! If the bottom block is lying on a tippy place then you won't be able to build the tower very high. After you have the bottom block in a good, solid place *(demonstrate),* what must you remember when you put the blocks on each other? *(Allow responses.)* Yes. Watch, and if I do it just right, I can make the tower higher and higher. *(Demonstrate.)* But each block must do its part to make the tower stand. What would happen if that block *(point to one near the middle of the tower you have built)* was tippy or would fall out? *(Allow responses.)* Right. The tower needs every block to stand up nicely.

Did you know that families are like towers? A family can stay happy and strong only if every member helps. If you don't help to make your home a nice place to be, if you make a mess and don't help to clean it up, or if you talk back and don't do what your father and mother ask you to do, do you know what you would be like? *(Allow responses.)*

You would be like a tippy block in the tower. If just one block doesn't do its part, the whole tower will fall down. Watch what happens if one block comes out of place. *(Pull out one of the blocks near the bottom and watch the whole tower fall.)*

We all need to do our part to make our homes happy and strong, and we all need to do our part to make our church happy and strong, too. We can do our part by loving Jesus and each other.

Jesus told his disciples the same thing. In John 15:12 he says, "Love each other as I have loved you." Let's learn that verse today.

I'll say it, and you say it back to me just like an echo. After that we'll ask our moms and dads and everyone else to say it all together with us. Ready? "Love each other as I have loved you." *(Encourage children to say verse.)* John 15, verse 12. *(Children echo.)* Now everyone. *(Lead all in saying verse and location.)*

It was the night before Jesus died that he told his disciples: "Love each other as I have loved you." *(Rebuild tower while ending lesson.)* If we do love one another as Jesus wants us to, we will help make our homes and our church strong just like a tower of building blocks that is solid and straight and strong.

32

God's Way Is the Best Way

Concept: Doing wrong things can stretch your conscience.

Object: A balloon

Memory Verse: Psalm 25:4—Show me your ways, O LORD, teach me your paths.

Look what I'm going to do! *(Show the children the balloon and blow it up part way.)* The first time you blow up a balloon it can be quite hard to do because the rubber is new. If I let this *(show balloon opening)* loose a little, what will happen?" *(Allow responses, then let the air out.)* Yes, it went flat, didn't it? I'll try to blow it up again. *(Do so, making it a little bigger this time.)* There. It was a little easier to blow up this time. Now I'll let the air out again. *(Do so.)* Look at the balloon now. *(Show how the rubber has stretched.)* See how the balloon is bigger than it used to be even though it doesn't have air in it?

Now I'll try it again. *(Blow it up a third time and make it a little larger than before.)* Did you notice that each time I blew the balloon up I made it a little bit bigger? Each time it got easier for me to blow it up too. Maybe if I did it one or two more times, I could make it so big it would pop. I had better not do that.

Instead *(let air out again),* I would like to have you look at the balloon now. It's not as stretchy as it was at first. It's really just kind of saggy and soft.

Did you know that God gave you and me something we call a conscience? A conscience is something inside of us like a little voice that tells us if what we are doing is right or wrong.

The first time we do something that our conscience tells us is wrong, we look to see if anyone is watching us and we feel scared. But the next time we do the same wrong thing, doing it doesn't bother us as much as it did before.

Our conscience gets stretched just like this balloon. Every time I blew up the balloon it was easier, and when I let the air out it didn't go back like it was before.

It's awfully dangerous to start doing wrong things, because every time you do, it's easier to do them again and again. Your conscience will be all stretched out, and it won't be able to tell you not to do wrong things. It will be like a balloon that gets so stretched out that it pops. You'll be in real trouble because you didn't listen to your conscience the first time.

A Bible verse that helps us listen to our conscience is Psalm 25:4. It says, "Show me your ways, O Lord, teach me your paths." Let's learn that verse today.

I'll say the first part, and you say it after me. Then I'll say the rest, and you say that back to me just like an echo. After that we'll ask our moms and dads and everyone else to say it all together with us. Ready? "Show me your ways, O Lord" *(encourage children to echo phrase),* "teach me your paths." *(Children echo.)* Psalm 25, verse 4. *(Children echo.)* Now everyone. *(Lead all in saying verse and location.)*

Whenever you see a balloon, boys and girls *(hold yours up),* try to remember to walk in God's ways. Listen to the little voice inside you that tells you what's right and what's wrong. Don't let your conscience get stretched out like an old balloon. Remember that God's way is always the best way.

33

The Bible Can Straighten Out Our Problems

Concept: God's laws straighten out mixed up situations.

Objects: A comb, messy hair, a small mirror

Memory Verse: Psalm 27:11—Teach me your way, O LORD, lead me in a straight path.

I'm sure all of you know what this is. *(Hold up the comb.)* Yes, it's a comb. I'm sure all of you know what it is used for too, don't you? *(Allow responses.)* Yes, if your hair is tangled when you get up in the morning or after a shower, you can untangle it and make it look right again if you comb it. Look at my hair. Do you think I combed my hair before coming to church? *(Allow responses.)* Well, I think I'll use this comb and straighten out my hair. *(Use the small mirror to help.)* Now, girls and boys, I would like to have you look at this comb with me. Notice that it has straight parts fastened to the back. We call these straight parts the teeth of the comb. They go through the tangled hair and put all of the hair in the right place again. They don't go from side to side or bend. They go straight through.

There are lots of tangled spots in our lives too. Boys and girls sometimes quarrel together. In our homes and in our schools, when we work and when we play, things sometimes can get quite tangled up.

What can we use as a comb to straighten out these problems? The answer is the Bible. In the Bible God gave us laws that don't bend all over. Instead, they straighten out our troubles and help us keep out of trouble.

That's why we come to church too. We come to learn God's Word so it can act like the straight teeth of a comb to untangle the problems in our lives and keep us out of trouble with one another.

Let's learn a verse from Psalm 27 today. Verse 11 shows us how to keep from getting all tangled up in sin. It says, "Teach me your way, O LORD, lead me in a straight path."

I'll say the first part, and you say it after me. Then I'll say the rest, and you say that back to me just like an echo. After that we'll ask our moms and dads and everyone else to say it all together with us. Ready? "Teach me your way, O LORD" *(encourage children to echo phrase),* "lead me in a straight path." *(Children echo.)* Psalm 27, verse 11. *(Children echo.)* Now everyone. *(Lead all in saying verse and location.)*

Whenever you use a comb to get the tangles out of your hair *(hold up comb),* remember that God teaches us, through his Word, to keep our lives untangled and straight. If our lives do get tangled up, we should use the Bible like a comb to get everything straightened out again.

Reaping What You Sow

Concept: Sowing good deeds helps you to enjoy good results later.

Objects: Seeds, small plant containers with different plants growing in them. (Note: A few weeks before you use this lesson, plant a few bean or pumpkin seeds in one small container; plant wheat, rye, lawn grass seed or other seeds that have a noticeably different leaf shape in the other. When these have grown large enough so that the different leaf shapes can easily be seen, they will be ready for the lesson.)

Memory Verse: Galatians 6:7—Do not be deceived: God cannot be mocked. A man reaps what he sows.

Today, boys and girls, I would like to show you some seeds. This first kind is rather large and flat. What kind of seed do you think this is? *(Allow responses.)* Those were good guesses. They are the seeds of a bean *(or whatever you planted)* plant. Now here is another kind of seed. What kind of seed do you think this is? *(Allow responses.)* When God created the world he made all kinds of different plants. Each plant has its own kind of seed. When we plant a bean seed, we get a bean plant. Just look at this plant. *(Show the plant.)* Now look at this plant. *(Show the other one.)* The plant looks very different because the seed I planted was different.

That is part of God's wonderful plan for the plants of the world. But that's part of God's plan for our lives too. The Bible tell us that if we do bad deeds, our lives will be bad. The Bible tells us that if we do good deeds, our lives will be good. We can't expect to have good lives if we plant bad deeds. Galatians 6:7 tells us this will always be true. It says, "Do not be deceived: God cannot be mocked. A man reaps what he sows." Let's learn it together.

I'll say the first part, and you say it after me. Then I'll say the rest, and you say that back to me just like an echo. After that we'll ask our moms and dads and everyone else to say it all together with us. Ready? "Do not be deceived: God cannot be mocked" *(encourage children to echo phrase)*. "A man reaps what he sows." *(Children echo.)* Galatians 6, verse 7. *(Children echo.)* Now everyone. *(Lead all in saying verse and location.)*

When people try to mock God, they make fun of him and don't do what he says because they think he doesn't really mean what he tells us to do in the Bible. But he does. What God says will always be true. He said if we plant one kind of seed, we will get that kind of a plant. *(Hold up a seed and its plant.)* Our deeds are like seeds. If we plant good deeds now, we will get good results later on in our lives.

35

Using God's Gifts

Concept: Christians should use the gifts God gives them in service of others.

Object: A gift-wrapped box

Memory Verse: 1 Peter 4:10—Each one should use whatever gift he has received to serve others.

D o any of you girls or boys know what this is? *(Hold up box.)* It's a box wrapped up like a gift. I didn't put anything in it. I want you to think about what you do with the gifts you receive. If your grandma gave you a toy, what do you suppose you would do with it? *(Allow responses.)* Suppose that you hardly played with it at all; what would that tell your grandma about how well you liked her present? *(Allow responses.)* Yes, that's right. Then suppose you picked out a special blouse for your mother's birthday and she hardly ever wore it. Would you think she liked it very much? *(Allow responses.)*

Did you know that God gave gifts to each of his children? To some he gave the gift to be helpers. Others have the gift to speak or pray very well. We all need to ask ourselves, "What kind of special gift or ability did God give me?" Sometimes we need to try to do different things before we find out how we can serve God best. Then we all need to remember what the Bible tells us about gifts in 1 Peter 4:10: "Each one should use whatever gift he has received to serve others." Let's learn that verse today.

I'll say it, and then you say it after me just like an echo. After that we'll ask our moms and dads and everyone else to say it all together with us. Ready? "Each one should use whatever gift he has received to serve others." *(Encourage children to say verse.)* First Peter 4, verse 10. *(Children echo.)* Now everyone. *(Lead all in saying verse and location.)*

If you gave someone something for Christmas *(hold up gift)* and that person never used it, you would think that person didn't like it very much. God gives us gifts too. The best way we have of showing him that we love him and appreciate his gifts is to use the gifts he gives us to serve others. Let's try to do that.

Part Eight
Growing in Faith

36

Following Directions

Concept: Following God's commandments
helps us grow in faith.

Object: Picture of parachutes

Memory Verse: John 14:15—If you love me,
you will obey what I command.

Look at this picture, boys and girls; what do you see? *(Hold up the picture. Allow responses.)* Right. When a person jumps out of an airplane high in the sky, he needs to have a parachute strapped to his back. After falling for awhile, what must he do? *(Allow responses.)* Good. A person who jumps out of an airplane with a parachute needs to follow directions very carefully. First the parachuter needs to know how to fold the parachute inside the pack just right so it will unfold the way it should. Then the parachuter needs to follow directions about pulling the cord. If he doesn't follow the directions, he is in big trouble!

The Bible gives us lots of directions about how to live. It tells us what to do to please God and how to show our love for others. John 14:15 says, "If you love me, you will obey what I command." Let's learn that important verse today.

I'll say it, and you say it after me just like an echo. After that we'll ask our moms and dads and everyone else to say it all together with us. Ready? "If you love me, you will obey what I command." *(Encourage children to say verse.)* John 14, verse 15. *(Children echo.)* Now everyone. *(Lead all in saying verse and location.)*

Imagine that you had jumped out of an airplane and were falling down toward the earth far below with a parachute strapped on your back. Then suppose that you thought, "Well, I know that the directions tell me to pull the cord so that the parachute will open, but I don't think I want to do what the directions tell me to do." Do you know what would happen? You would be killed. You would be killed because you didn't do what you were supposed to do.

The parachuter shows that he is obedient to the directions by pulling the cord that will save his life. He shows his faith in the parachute and trusts that it will open. If we obey the commandments that God gives us in the Bible, we show our faith and trust in him too.

We will find the most happiness if we do what God tells us to do. Just like the parachuter who follows the direction to pull the cord *(show the picture),* obeying God's commandments is the best thing for us to do.

37

Believing without Seeing

Concept: We have to believe in Jesus without seeing him.

Objects: Blindfold and an apple

Memory Verse: John 20:29—Because you have seen me, you have believed; blessed are those who have not seen and yet have believed.

I need a volunteer to be blindfolded; who will help me? *(Allow responses.)* Before I put the blindfold over your eyes, I want you to look at the apple over on the piano *(or other nearby obvious place)*. Do you see the apple? *(Allow response.)* Good! I'm going to put this blindfold over your eyes now. *(Do so, then ask if the child can see or not to be sure the blindfold is in place.)* Next I need to pick out another volunteer to help me too. *(Allow responses. Pick out another child but do not place a blindfold on this child.)* I need to ask you the same question that I asked (blindfolded child): Do you see the apple and where it is? *(Allow response.)* Now I'm going to ask (blindfolded child) again. Where is the apple? *(Allow response.)* Right! Now I'm going to move the apple someplace else. There, (unblindfolded child), can you tell me where the apple is now? *(Allow response.)* Yes, I moved the apple to the chair. (<u>Blindfolded child</u>), can you tell me where you think the apple is now? *(Allow response.)* Yes, it's on the chair. But you can't see it, so how do you know it's on the chair? *(Allow response.)* Yes, because (<u>unblindfolded child</u>) and I both said it was. *(Remove the blindfold and thank participants.)*

Some people today say that seeing is believing. They say they won't believe anything is true unless they see it themselves. (<u>Blindfolded child</u>) believed the apple was on the chair instead of the piano because (<u>unblindfolded child</u>) and I both said it was. He (she) believed it because of what someone else said.

When Jesus had risen from the grave, he came to see his disciples but Thomas was not there. When the others told Thomas they had seen Jesus, he said he wouldn't believe it unless he saw Jesus with his own eyes. Later Jesus came to his disciples again and this time Thomas was with them. Then Thomas believed Jesus had really risen from the grave. In John 20:29 we can find what Jesus said to Thomas. He said, "Because you have seen me, you have believed; blessed are those who have not seen and yet have believed." Let's learn that verse today.

I'll say the first part, and you say it after me. Then I'll say the rest, and you say that back to me just like an echo. After that we'll ask our moms and dads and everyone else to say it all together with us. Ready? "Because you have seen me, you have believed" *(encourage children to echo phrase);* "blessed are those who have not seen and yet have believed." *(Children echo.)* John 20, verse 29. *(Children echo.)* Now every-one. *(Lead all in saying verse and location.)*

Jesus made sure that verse was in the Bible for people like us, boys and girls. We haven't seen Jesus after he arose from the grave like the disciples did. We just have to believe that what the Bible tells us is true. And everyone who does believe that Jesus really is alive is truly blessed.

38

Praying Hands

Concept: We use our hands in prayer and in service.

Object: A statue of praying hands

Memory Verse: 1 Thessalonians 5:17–18—
Pray continually; give thanks in all
circumstances.

Look at this, boys and girls *(hold up the statue).* Do you know what this is? *(Allow responses.)* Good! I don't know where the rest of the person is; it's only a statue of someone's hands. They are the hands of someone who is praying. How do you hold your hands when you pray? *(Allow responses.)* Yes, most of the time when we pray we fold our hands to show that we depend on God to answer our prayer. We don't play with things while we pray because that would keep us from really thinking about God.

In 1 Thessalonians 5:17–18 the Bible tells us to pray continually. That's a really important thing for us to remember. Let's learn those verses today.

I'll say the first part, and you say it after me. Then I'll say the rest, and you say that back to me just like an echo. After that we'll ask our moms and dads and everyone else to say it all together with us. Ready? "Pray continually" *(encourage children to echo phrase);* "give thanks in all circumstances." *(Children echo.)* First Thessalonians 5, verses 17 and 18. *(Children echo.)* Now everyone. *(Lead all in saying verse and location.)*

Look at your hands. Hands are good for lots of things. They help you clap for joy. They help you do the work you need to do for your mom and dad. They help you eat and put on your clothes. They even help you tie your shoes. But best of all, they help you to pray. *(Hold up the statue.)* When the Bible tells us to pray continually, it means we should always be talking with God. We can talk to him silently in our hearts while we do lots of different things. We also need those times when we sit quietly, fold our hands, and talk to God. God is always ready to hear and answer our prayers. What a wonderful way to use our hands for Jesus.

Learning from (

Concept: Imitate the

Object: A parakeet (
 lesson you will nee
 has a parakeet you can bring to church.)

Memory Verse: Hebrews 13:7—Consider the
 outcome of their way of life and imitate
 their faith.

 Today we have a special friend with us. His
name is (<u>name of the parakeet</u>). He is really nice.
What kinds of things do you think he can do? *(Allow
responses.)* Yes, parakeets can do lots of interesting
things. Did you know that parakeets are like small
parrots? Some parrots can be taught to say words.
You can teach a parrot to say, "Polly want a cracker?"
Some parakeets can learn to say some words too. *(If
the one you have can do so, encourage it to do so or to
make other sounds.)* Can a parrot or a parakeet really
make up words or sentences to say? *(Allow responses.)*
Right; they just imitate you. To imitate someone
means to say what another person says or do what
another person does. Did you know that the Bible
talks about imitating others? In the Book of Hebrews
the Bible tells us about lots of people who loved and

tells us about Abel and Noah, about Moses, and about many others. In chapter, verse 7 it tells us to think about the lives of people and to imitate them. It says, "Consider the outcome of their way of life and imitate their faith." Let's learn that verse today.

I'll say the first part, and you say it after me. Then I'll say the rest, and you say that back to me just like an echo. After that we'll ask our moms and dads and everyone else to say it all together with us. Ready? "Consider the outcome of their way of life" *(encourage children to echo phrase)* "and imitate their faith." *(Children echo.)* Hebrews 13, verse 7. *(Children echo.)* Now everyone. *(Lead all in saying verse and location.)*

About the only way our parakeet can learn to talk or make new sounds is to listen to someone else make them first. Then it will try to make the same sounds, to imitate the sounds, that someone else has made. One good way for us to help our faith grow is to look at the lives of other Christians who have strong faith. Then we need to do what they do. Let's look for good examples in the Bible, in the church, and in our families. Then let's try to follow their example and live good lives too.

40

Wise Choices

Concept: Choose to do what God would have you do.

Object: Picture of many kinds of ice-cream cones

Memory Verse: Joshua 24:15—Choose for yourselves this day whom you will serve. . . . But as for me and my household, we will serve the LORD.

Look at these pictures of ice-cream cones, boys and girls. Let's imagine that it's a hot summer afternoon and you have just enough money to buy one ice-cream cone. Then suppose that you go past an ice cream store that has twenty-eight different flavors. Which flavor would you choose? *(Allow responses. You may want to call on the children one at a time so all get a chance to answer.)*

That would be a hard decision for me because there are so many to choose from. We have to make lots of other choices too. Every time we turn on the T.V. we have to make a choice. We have to choose between good programs and bad programs. Which one should we choose? *(Allow responses.)* Yes, we have to choose the best ones. Our parents often help us choose those that are best. Sometimes we even have to choose to turn off the T.V. because none of the programs are good.

Sometimes you have to choose between playing with one friend or another friend. If one friend asks you to play ball and another friend asks you to go for a hike, you have to choose. You can't do both at the same time. Life is full of choices. Every day you have new choices to make. This was true long ago when God's people, Israel, didn't worship God very much anymore. Instead they began to worship idols. Then Joshua asked them to make a choice. In the Bible in Joshua 24:15 we read these words: "Choose for yourselves this day whom you will serve. . . . But as for me and my household, we will serve the LORD." Let's learn those words today as our memory verse to remind ourselves to make good choices.

I'll say the first part, and you say it after me. Then I'll say the rest, and you say that back to me just like an echo. After that we'll ask our moms and dads and everyone else to say it all together with us. Ready? "Choose for yourselves this day whom you will serve. . . ." *(encourage children to echo phrase)* "But as for me and my household, we will serve the LORD." *(Children echo.)* Joshua 24, verse 15. *(Children echo.)* Now everyone. *(Lead all in saying verse and location.)*

Joshua asked the people to choose if they were going to serve God or idols. Then he told them that he and his family had chosen to serve God. What an important choice to make! If you aren't for God, you are against him. We all have choices to make. *(Hold up the picture of the ice-cream cones.)* Our most important choice is to choose to serve God. During this coming week find a way every day to show that you have chosen to serve God.

Part Nine
Christian Virtues

41

Give a Gentle Answer

Concept: One way to be a peacemaker is to give a gentle answer instead of speaking harsh words.

Object: A referee's whistle

Memory Verse: Proverbs 15:1—A gentle answer turns away wrath, but a harsh word stirs up anger.

I have something in my hands *(keep whistle inside your cupped hands),* and I'm going to put it to my mouth. I want you to listen and tell me what I'm holding. *(Blow the whistle without letting the children see it. Allow responses.)* Right! It's a referee's whistle. When basketball players play a game, a person called a referee has a whistle like this. Do you know when he blows the whistle? *(Allow responses.)* Yes, when a player does something he or she isn't supposed to do, the referee blows the whistle like this *(do so again).* Did you ever wonder what would happen if there were no referees? Well, I think the ball game would get rougher and rougher, and pretty soon everybody would be fighting and yelling. This little whistle helps keep peace between the teams.

Sometimes people who aren't playing basketball get angry at each other too. They may say harsh or angry words to each other. If someone says something to you in an angry voice, what should you do? Should you say something angry right back? *(Allow responses.)* That would be a sure way to start a fight.

The Bible tells us how we should reply when someone says something in a harsh and angry voice to us. In Proverbs 15:1 we read: "A gentle answer turns away wrath, but a harsh word stirs up anger." "Wrath" means anger. Let's learn that verse today.

I'll say the first part, and you say it after me. Then I'll say the rest, and you say that back to me just like an echo. After that we'll ask our moms and dads and everyone else to say it all together with us. Ready? "A gentle answer turns away wrath" *(encourage children to echo phrase)*, "but a harsh word stirs up anger." *(Children echo.)* Proverbs 15, verse 1. *(Children echo.)* Now everyone. *(Lead all in saying verse and location.)*

If someone says something that is unkind or angry to you, the first thing you feel like doing is saying something unkind or angry right back. But God tells us we mustn't do that. When people say mean things to you, the best thing to do is just wait for a minute before answering. Think of the referee's whistle blowing. *(Blow the whistle.)* Then say something gentle. Say a kind thing back to them instead. If you do that, you'll be a peacemaker. You'll be the kind of person that God wants you to be.

42

Showing Compassion

> **Concept:** Showing compassion means that
> we "suffer with" others.
>
> **Object:** A bandaged toe with an imagined
> injury (or someone with a real injury)
>
> **Memory Verse:** Zechariah 7:9—This is what
> the LORD Almighty says: . . ."show mercy
> and compassion to one another."

Did you ever have a really sore toe or sore
knee? *(Hold up your bandaged toe. Allow responses.)*
Well, I'm just pretending I've got a reeeeally sore toe.
Let's imagine that if I hold it down it throbs every
time my heart beats. If it was really hurt I would hold
it up when I could so it wouldn't hurt quite as much.
How many of you feel sorry for me? *(Allow responses.)*
Thank you. Once when I really had a sore toe, a few
grown-ups kind of smiled about it. When I told them
I had kicked a chair walking through the kitchen
without putting on a light, one person even laughed
a little. It was kind of a stupid thing to do, but it still
hurt.

How do you act when you see other people who
are hurting or sad or sick or lonely? The Bible tells
us that we must have compassion on them. "Com-

passion" is a big word, isn't it? Let's say it together: COMPASSION. The word "compassion" means "to suffer with." If we know of someone who is hurting, as Christians we should suffer with them.

Long ago the Indians believed that to understand someone else's feelings, you had to walk in his or her moccasins for a time. That is, you had to feel what that person felt. If he or she were suffering you had to learn to suffer like that too. In the Old Testament God tells us to have mercy and to show compassion. Zechariah 7:9 tells us: "This is what the LORD Almighty says: . . .'show mercy and compassion to one another.'" Let's learn that verse today.

I'll say the first part, and you say it after me. Then I'll say the rest, and you say that back to me just like an echo. After that we'll ask our moms and dads and everyone else to say it all together with us. Ready? "This is what the LORD Almighty says" *(encourage children to echo phrase):* "'. . . show mercy and compassion to one another.'" *(Children echo.)* Zechariah 7, verse 9. *(Children echo.)* Now everyone. *(Lead all in saying verse and location.)*

I'm so glad you said you would feel sorry for me if I really had a sore toe. *(Hold up the toe.)* Do you know that the boys and girls who felt the most sorry for me are the ones who have had a sore toe themselves? That's because they "suffer with" me. The Bible tells us to have compassion, to suffer with others who suffer. Let's try to do that! It will really help them.

43

Following the Golden Rule

Concept: Treat others as nicely as you would like to have them treat you.

Objects: A gold watch, a silver watch, a plastic watch

Memory Verse: Matthew 7:12—In everything, do to others what you would have them do to you.

Today, girls and boys, I brought with me a few watches. Look at this one first. It has a black plastic case and band. *(Hold it up.)* Now look at this one. It's silver. *(Hold it up.)* The case is silver and so is the band. Which one do you think cost more money? *(Allow responses.)* Yes, the silver watch *(hold it up)* is the more expensive one. Now I'd like to have you look at this gold watch. *(Hold it up next to the silver one.)* Which of these two, the silver or the gold, do you think cost more? *(Allow responses.)* Right. The gold one is more valuable; gold is a very precious metal. People use gold to make rings and other expensive jewelry. We use iron to make shovels and rakes to work in the garden, and we use a metal like aluminum to make pots and pans. We don't use gold to make ordinary things because gold is too precious.

In the Bible there is a rule that we call the "Golden Rule" because it is one of the most precious rules in God's Word. Do you know what that rule tells us to do? It's found in Matthew 7:12. It says, "In everything, do to others what you would have them do to you." Let's use that verse as our memory work today.

I'll say the first part, and you say it after me. Then I'll say the rest, and you say that back to me just like an echo. After that we'll ask our moms and dads and everyone else to say it all together with us. Ready? "In everything, do to others" *(encourage children to echo phrase)* "what you would have them do to you." *(Children echo.)* Matthew 7, verse 12. *(Children echo.)* Now everyone. *(Lead all in saying verse and location.)*

What kinds of things would you like to have other people do to you? The Bible says that if you want them to say nice things to you, you must say nice things to them. The Bible says that if you want them to be nice to you, you must be nice to them. Every time you see something that is made of gold *(hold up the gold watch),* think of how precious this rule from the Bible is. If we would always treat others as nicely as we would like to have them treat us, what a wonderful place this world would be.

44

Are You Tired?

Concept: Don't give up on doing good even if you are tired.

Object: Picture of runners in a race

Memory Verse: Galatians 6:9—Let us not become weary in doing good, for at the proper time we will reap a harvest if we do not give up.

Today I have a picture for you to look at. *(Hold up the picture.)* It's a picture of some runners running a race. Have you ever run a race? *(Allow responses.)* What do you have to do to win a race? *(Allow responses.)* Yes, you have to run faster than everyone else. There are different kinds of races. Some races are for short distances. The runners run as fast as they can for a quarter of a mile or so. When they finish, they are puffing and are quite tired because they ran as fast as they could.

Another kind of race is the long-distance race. In this kind of race the runners need to run miles and miles. Cross-country runners who run for miles and miles have to set a pace. They run at a certain speed that's not too fast. Then when they're almost to the

112

end, they speed up to the finish line. Such runners who run many miles must get very tired.

The Bible in Galatians 6:9 tells us not to grow weary, but it isn't talking about getting tired when you run a race. It's talking about not getting tired of doing good things. It says, "Let us not become weary in doing good, for at the proper time we will reap a harvest if we do not give up." Let's learn that verse today.

I'll say the first part, and you say it after me. Then I'll say the rest, and you say that back to me just like an echo. After that we'll ask our moms and dads and everyone else to say it all together with us. Ready? "Let us not become weary in doing good" *(encourage children to echo phrase),* "for at the proper time we will reap a harvest if we do not give up." *(Children echo.)* Galatians 6, verse 9. *(Children echo.)* Now everyone. *(Lead all in saying verse and location.)*

Sometimes you can get very tired of doing good things for other people. Maybe it is just the hard work you have to do. Maybe you wash windows for sick people or mow their lawns. Maybe you get tired of doing things for others because they don't seem to appreciate your good deeds. Well, the Bible tells us that doing good is something like running a race. It makes you tired and you may feel like quitting. But the Bible also tells us not to give up and quit. Instead it tells us to keep doing good things because if we do we will reap the harvest, that is, we'll win. We will receive God's blessings at the end of the race. So don't give up doing good things even if you are tired. Do them anyway because God asks you to.

45

As Faithful As "Old Faithful"

Concept: Christians need to be faithful.

Object: Picture of "Old Faithful" geyser

Memory Verse: Revelation 2:10—Be faithful, even to the point of death, and I will give you the crown of life.

Today I have a picture to show you, girls and boys. It's a picture of "Old Faithful," a geyser. *(Hold up the picture.)* Have any of you ever seen a geyser? *(Allow responses. If someone has been to Yellowstone National Park and has seen "Old Faithful" have the child describe it. If no one has actually seen it, the group may be able to describe it from having seen it on T.V.)*

When a geyser erupts, it blows hot water up in a big stream like a fountain. You have to stay far enough away, because the water is really hot. Scientists think that steam and pressure in the ground are what cause geysers to shoot hot water up into the air. There are many geysers in different parts of the world. A geyser in New Zealand once blew hot water up fifteen hundred feet into the air. "Giant Geyser" in Yellowstone National Park once blew out almost a million gallons of water in one eruption. But this is a picture of "Old Faithful." *(Hold up the picture.)* Do

114

any of you know why this geyser was given a name like that? *(Allow responses.)* Yes, park rangers keep track of when "Old Faithful" erupts and then they know almost exactly when it will erupt again. They put that time up on a bulletin board so visitors can see "Old Faithful" blow up a fountain of hot water and steam.

Faithfulness is important. Bus drivers need to be faithful because day after day they need to make stops at almost exactly the same time. You can depend on them. Your mother is faithful to you. She has meals ready for you to eat. She doesn't take care of you one day and forget about you the next day. No, she's faithful. You can depend on her.

There's a verse in the Bible that tells us that Christians should be faithful. It's found in Revelation 2:10. It says, "Be faithful, even to the point of death, and I will give you the crown of life." Let's learn that verse today.

I'll say the first part, and you say it after me. Then I'll say the rest, and you say that back to me just like an echo. After that we'll ask our moms and dads and everyone else to say it all together with us. Ready? "Be faithful, even to the point of death" *(encourage children to echo phrase),* "and I will give you the crown of life." *(Children echo.)* Revelation 2, verse 10. *(Children echo.)* Now everyone. *(Lead all in saying verse and location.)*

Being a faithful Christian is really important. We can't be a Christian one day and not the next. We can't be kind and obedient on Sunday and not on Monday or the other days of the week. To be faithful is to be kind and obedient every day. We need to live like Christians every day. When can we quit being faithful? Our verse tells us to be faithful all of our lives up to the time we die. Then Jesus will give us a heavenly crown of life. Think of "Old Faithful" *(hold up the picture)* and remember to be a faithful Christian.

Part Ten

Heaven

46

Put Your Treasures
in a Safe Place

Concept: Instead of earthly possessions, store up heavenly treasures.

Objects: Piggy bank and pennies

Memory Verse: Matthew 6:21—For where your treasure is, there your heart will be also.

Some of you may have one of these. *(Hold up the piggy bank.)* Do you know what it is? *(Allow responses.)* Yes, it's a bank that looks like a pig *(or whatever the shape)*. On the top, there is a narrow opening. What is that for? *(Allow responses.)* Yes. Let me try it. *(Drop in a few pennies.)* The opening is so small, I can't get my fingers in to get the pennies out again. What if I need the money to buy something? *(Allow responses.)* I could shake the money out, or I could break the bank, but I wouldn't want to do that. Look at the bottom. *(Show the bottom of the bank.)* If I open that, I can get the money out. *(Demonstrate.)* Then I could spend my money. All my savings would be gone and I would have to start saving all over again.

Did you know that the Bible talks about saving? Jesus told us to lay up treasures in heaven. That sounds hard, but Jesus tells us how. It's like putting pennies in a bank. Jesus tells us to do kind things for others. Those things will be stored up in heaven, just as our pennies are stored in our banks. People think a lot about how much money they have saved. If we do that, we begin to love the money and other things we have more than we love God. Matthew 6:21 says, "For where your treasure is, there your heart will be also." Let's learn that verse today so we will always remember it.

I'll say the first part, and you say it after me. Then I'll say the rest, and you say that back to me just like an echo. After that we'll ask our moms and dads and everyone else to say it all together with us. Ready? "For where your treasure is" *(encourage children to echo phrase)*, "there your heart will be also." *(Children echo.)* Matthew 6, verse 21. *(Children echo.)* Now everyone. *(Lead all in saying verse and location.)*

The treasures we have on earth get old. Clothes wear out. Houses need new roofs. Cars get rusty. Jesus told us not to love earthly things so much that we forget about God, who made it possible for us to have them. If we do love earthly treasures so much, Jesus said, we are storing up treasures in the wrong place.

You certainly may save your pennies in a bank like this *(hold up bank)*, and you may enjoy all the wonderful blessings God gives you, but always remember to give God first place in your life. Love him more than anything else and do what he asks you to do; then you'll always have treasures in heaven.

47

Our Father's House Has Many Rooms

Concept: Heaven has room for all of God's family.

Objects: A dollhouse, pictures of houses of different sizes from a real estate brochure, a picture of the White House

Memory Verse: John 14:2—In my Father's house are many rooms; if it were not so, I would have told you. I am going there to prepare a place for you.

I would like to have you look at this dollhouse. How many rooms do you think it has? *(Allow responses.)* Actually it has (<u>correct number</u>). Some real houses have many rooms and some have just a few. Look at a few of the houses in these pictures. Here's a picture of a big one. The advertisement says it has (<u>number</u>) rooms. One of the most important houses in our country is the president's house, called the White House. How many rooms do you think there are in the White House? *(Allow responses. Show the picture.)* The White House has 132 rooms. Some hotels in large cities have hundreds of rooms. I guess the reason some houses and hotels have so many rooms is so that they can have lots of guests. *(If you know of a prominent or historic home in your area, you may wish to tell how many rooms it has.)*

Some of you have a bedroom all to yourself and others share a bedroom with a brother or sister. Some people have an empty bedroom that is just used when somebody comes to stay overnight.

When your grandma and grandpa come for a visit or you have some friends sleep overnight, you may run out of bedrooms. You may have to sleep in a sleeping bag on the floor. Then you may wish your house had more rooms.

The day before Jesus was crucified, he told his disciples about heaven. Jesus knew how big heaven was because he was there before he came to earth. He wanted his disciples and us to know that heaven has plenty of room for all of God's family. When he explained this to his disciples, he said, "In my Father's house are many rooms; if it were not so, I would have told you. I am going there to prepare a place for you." That is John 14:2. Let's learn this verse today.

I'll say the first part, and you say it after me. Then I'll say the rest, and you say that back to me just like an echo. After that we'll ask our moms and dads and everyone else to say it all together with us. Ready? "In my Father's house are many rooms" *(encourage children to echo phrase);* "if it were not so, I would have told you." *(Children echo.)* "I am going there to prepare a place for you." *(Children echo.)* John 14, verse 2. *(Children echo.)* Now everyone. *(Lead all in saying verse and location.)*

Some of our houses have many rooms; some have just a few. *(Hold up the pictures.)* Whether there are many or few, if the people who live in the house love each other and are kind to one another it will be a happy home. Jesus has promised that he is preparing enough rooms in our heavenly home so that there will be room for all of God's family. We can be sure that it will be filled with love and joy forever because we will be there with Jesus.

48

Talking the Same Language

Concept: In heaven we will meet people of every race and language.

Object: Tape of a foreign language

Memory Verse: Revelation 7:9—I looked and there was a great multitude that no one could count, from every nation, tribe, people and language, standing before the throne.

Today I brought my tape player with me. I would like to have you listen to a tape. *(Play the tape for a short time.)* What was the speaker saying? *(Allow responses.)* I'm not surprised that you can't understand what the person is saying, because he's speaking in Japanese *(or whatever the language is).* I can't understand it either. Did you ever go to a store or to the airport where you heard people speaking in another language? *(Allow responses.)* I'm glad you did because now you know something about what happened long ago.

When God first made the world there was only one language. But then the people decided to build a big tower, the Tower of Babel. They wanted to stay in one place even though God had commanded them to spread all over the earth. Then God changed their one language into many different languages so they couldn't understand each other. Now there are Christians all over the world who believe in Jesus as their Savior but don't understand each other because they speak different languages.

Someday in heaven all of God's family will be gathered before Christ's throne. Revelation 7:9 tells us something about that great day in these words: "I looked and there was a great multitude that no one could count, from every nation, tribe, people and language, standing before the throne." Let's learn that verse today.

I'll say the first part, and you say it after me. Then I'll say the rest, and you say that back to me just like an echo. After that we'll ask our moms and dads and everyone else to say it all together with us. Ready? "I looked and there was a great multitude that no one could count" *(encourage children to echo phrase)*, "from every nation, tribe, people and language, standing before the throne." *(Children echo.)* Revelation 7, verse 9. *(Children echo.)* Now everyone. *(Lead all in saying verse and location.)*

What a great day that will be! In heaven we'll meet before Jesus' throne with God's family members of every color and language, and we'll all get along without any trouble. Wouldn't it be wonderful if people of all races and languages could start doing this on earth, just as it is done in heaven? Of course we don't understand everyone's language *(hold up the tape)* like we will in heaven, but we can still try to do God's will on earth by getting along with people of different colors and languages, especially those in God's family.

49

When Will Jesus Return?

Concept: We must be ready for Jesus' return.

Objects: Clock and calendar

Memory Verse: Matthew 25:13—Therefore keep watch, because you do not know the day or the hour.

Listen, boys and girls; can you hear this clock tick? *(Allow responses. If someone says no, hold the clock by his or her ear.)* What does the ticking of the clock mean? *(Allow responses.)* Yes, it tells us that the seconds, the minutes, and the hours are slowly but surely going by. Now look at this calendar. Today is Sunday, (today's date). Who can point to today's date on my calendar? *(Allow responses. Choose one or several to do so.)* Good. We said that the ticking clock showed that seconds, minutes, and hours are going by. The calendar shows that days and months and years are going by too. When times goes by it never comes back again. So we always have to be aware of the time that is coming. We need to get ready for the things that are going to happen.

Let's imagine that Grandma is going to pick us up at three o'clock, or a friend is coming for supper at six, or the school bus is coming at eight o'clock. We need to be on time for things like that. The more important a meeting is, the more important it is for us to be on time for it.

The most important thing that is ever going to happen is the return of Jesus from heaven back to earth. Then he will take us to heaven with him. He wants us to be ready for the time when he comes again. There is just one problem. We don't know just exactly when that will be. There is a verse in the Bible, Matthew 25:13, that says, "Therefore keep watch, because you do not know the day or the hour." Let's learn that verse today.

I'll say the first part, and you say it after me. Then I'll say the rest, and you say that back to me just like an echo. After that we'll ask our moms and dads and everyone else to say it all together with us. Ready? "Therefore keep watch" *(encourage children to echo phrase)*, "because you do not know the day or the hour." *(Children echo.)* Matthew 25, verse 13. *(Children echo.)* Now everyone. *(Lead all in saying verse and location.)*

No, we do not know what day Jesus is coming back from heaven. Nor do we know what time of the day he will come. How can we keep from being surprised by his return? Well, there's only one way and that is to be ready for him to come at any time! So don't do things that you wouldn't want to be caught doing when he comes again. When you see the hours go by on the clock or when you change the pages from month to month on the calendar, remember that Jesus is coming again. Always live the way he wants you to live so you will be ready to meet him!

50

There's Only One Door

Concept: Jesus is the only way to get to heaven.

Objects: A paper bag, a glass of water

Memory Verse: John 14:6—I am the way and the truth and the life. No one comes to the Father except through me.

Girls and boys, have you ever had the hiccups? *(Allow responses.)* Do you know what causes a person to get the hiccups? *(Allow responses.)* Well, do you know how to get over the hiccups? *(Allow responses.)* Right. One suggestion is that you slowly drink a glass of cold water like this to stop them. *(Demonstrate.)* Or maybe they would stop if you held your breath or if you breathed into a paper sack for a few minutes like this. *(Demonstrate.)* There are lots of ideas about how to stop the hiccups.

Sometimes even though you try lots of different ideas, you can't get rid of them. You just go right on "hicking." A man named Jack O'Leary holds the world record for having hiccups for the longest time. He had them for eight years, from 1948 to 1956. During that time, he hiccuped about 160,000,000 times. When he started he weighed 134 pounds but when he stopped

127

he only weighed 74 pounds. Lots of people tried to help him by sending him different ideas they thought would make his hiccups stop. People sent him over 60,000 suggestions to try to get over the problem. But ideas for cures don't always work.

People have lots of ideas for ways to get into heaven, too. Some people think you can get to heaven by earning your way, by doing good things all your life. Others say you just have to believe.

Long ago Jesus gave us the only possible way to get to heaven. It's written in the Bible in John 14:6: "I am the way and the truth and the life. No one comes to the Father except through me." Let's learn that very important verse today.

I'll say the first part, and you say it after me. Then I'll say the rest, and you say that back to me just like an echo. After that we'll ask our moms and dads and everyone else to say it all together with us. Ready? "I am the way and the truth and the life" *(encourage children to echo phrase).* "No one comes to the Father except through me." *(Children echo.)* John 14, verse 6. *(Children echo.)* Now everyone. *(Lead all in saying verse and location.)*

Lots of people tried to help Jack O'Leary when he had the hiccups for so long. All of those 60,000 ideas to stop the hiccups didn't cure him. *(Hold up the bag and water.)* People have all kinds of ideas about how we can get to heaven too. But the Bible tells us that believing in Jesus as our Savior is the only way to heaven. He invites us to come to heaven through faith in him!